Praise for

How Jane Austen Kept her Cool

AN A TO Z HISTORY OF GEORGIAN ICE CREAM

MARIA GRACE

White Soup Press

Published by: White Soup Press
How Jane Austen Kept her Cool: An A to Z
History of Georgian Ice Cream
Copyright © August 2018 Maria Grace

For information, address
author.MariaGrace@gmail.com

ISBN-13: 978-0-9980937-9-6 (White Soup Press)

Author's Website: RandomBitsofFaascination.com
Email address: Author.MariaGrace@gmail.com

Dedication

For my husband and sons.
You have always believed in me.

Table of Contents

CHAPTER 1

A Brief History of Ice Cream

But in the meantime, for elegance and ease and luxury, the Hattons and Milles' dine here to-day, and I shall eat ice and drink French wine, and be above vulgar economy.~ Jane Austen to Cassandra, Godmersham, June 20, 1808

We know Jane Austen ate ice cream, perhaps not regularly, but as a treat while visiting her wealthier connections. She clearly considered it a treat, an escape from the "vulgar economies" of day-to-day life.

It is easy to think of ice cream being a fairly recent development on the food scene, considering that it needs refrigeration in order to work after all, and *that* hasn't been around very long. The ice trade flourished during the Victorian era, making refrigeration possible, so that seems a likely era for the proliferation of frozen confections.

But hey, where there's a will there's a way. Ice cream is just too good to have waited that long. Human ingenuity crafted the pyramids with man power alone—ice cream sounds simple by comparison, doesn't it? So it shouldn't really be a surprise that ice cream has been around for a lot longer than we realize, hundreds, maybe thousands of years longer.

Ice Cream in the Ancient World

It is a little difficult to tell exactly who produced the first ice cream and from there how it actually got to Europe. But, first things first. Before you could have ice cream in the days before refrigeration, you had to have ice.

Mesopotamia boasted some of the earliest ice storage houses, in use about four thousand years ago. The wealthy—generally the only ones who had access to ice until refrigeration came on the scene—used the ice to cool their wine. A little later, Alexander the Great decided his army would appreciate chilled wine during the hot months, so he had pits dug and filled with snow to save for the summer. (Andrews, 2001) The idea appeared to catch on, and the Greeks sold snow in the fifth century BC markets of Athens.

When and where did we cross the line from using ice to make things cold to actually creating frozen foods? There seems to be two lines of thinking. Some food historians suggest the Chinese created the first ice creams, possibly as early as 3000 BC. (Olver, 2004). Others suggest it was several thousand years later, crediting the Tang Dynasty of the seventh, eighth and ninth centuries with mixing dairy products into a frozen confections. "Using milk from cows, goats, or buffalo, lowered into ice pools in metal tubes, this embryonic version of ice cream was a treat for emperors." (Rossen, 2017) Still others point to the Turkish Empire, where iced fruit drinks called sarbat were frequently consumed, as the originators of frozen confections of today. (Andrews, 2001)

Ice Cream goes to Europe

How did ice cream get to Europe? Culinary mythology suggests Marco Polo brought back the notion of water ices and frozen confections when he returned to Venice from his trip to China in the thirteenth century. However, Sicily (considered by some the Western world's home of frozen ices) claims an Arabic inspiration for these sweet treats. (Simeti, 1989) All in all, it is difficult to say whether water ices were first made in Italy, France or Spain. Regardless of where they originated, they did not take long to spread among the more sophisticated cities of Europe during the seventeenth century. (Davidson, 1999)

Italians were masters in developing methods of chilling and freezing drinks into sorbets and granitas. Latini's *Treatise on Various Kinds of Sorbets, or Water Ices* (written between 1692 and 1694) contained the first written recipes on how to mix sugar, salt, snow, fruits and their juices, as well as chocolate, and spices into a variety of frozen confections. The book also includes a "milk sorbet that is first cooked," which was probably the first true ice cream recipe. *De'sorbetti* by Filippo Baldini in 1775 was one of the first books entirely dedicated to frozen confections. An entire chapter dealt with "milky sorbets," (in other words ice creams) vigorously proclaiming their medicinal properties. (Capatti, 1999)

Ice Cream and the English Speaking World

The first record of ice cream in English is found on a 1671 menu for a feast for the Knights of the Garter at Windsor Castle. The earliest published recipe in English appeared in *Mrs. Eale's Receipts*, a book dedicated to confectionery printed in London in 1718.

From England, it was only a short hop for ice cream to appear across the pond in the United States. The earliest record of ice cream in the United States suggests it was served in 1744 by the lady of Governor Blandon of Maryland, nee Barbara Jannsen, daughter of Lord Baltimore. (Davidson, 1999) During the 1770's, George Washington helped popularize the dish, serving it at his estate, Mount Vernon, during elite functions. As president in 1790, merchant records suggest Washington spent over $200 ($3000 in today's prices) on ice cream during the summer. Presidents Jefferson and Madison also served ice cream for special occasions.

As ice cream continued to be served at elite functions and became more accessible for the populace, a national love affair with the confection began. "Authelme Brittat-Savarin, a French politician and writer on gastronomy, tells how a French Captain named Collet made and sold ices in New York in 1794 and 1795. He describes, with satisfaction, the surprise of American women at this technological and masculine feat: 'Nothing could be more amusing than the little grimaces they made when eating them. They were utterly at a loss to conceive how a substance could be kept so cold in a temperature of ninety degrees.'" (Stradley, 2017) (Yeah, I know you cringed upon reading that it was a "masculine feat," but remember it was written over two hundred years ago; so let's just move on from that.)

That brings us up to the Regency portion of the Georgian era, the time of Jane Austen. Before we move on though, how about a little quiz to see what you already know about Georgian era ice cream.

Ice Cream IQ

1. What flavor of ice cream would have most likely been Jane Austen's favorite?
   a. Chocolate
   b. Vanilla
   c. Rose-water
   d. Saffron

2. Ice cream cones were not invented until the early 1900's
   a. True
   b. False

3. Which of the following is the MOST important ingredient for making ice cream?
   a. Salt
   b. Cream
   c. Sugar

4. Jane Austen might have used a hand crank ice cream machine to make ice cream.
   a. True
   b. False

5. Jane Austen was likely to have bought ice cream from street peddlers.
   a. True
   b. False

6. Ice cream was sometimes molded into the

shape of meat, like a pig's head.
    a. True
    b. False

7. Ice cream and ices were always served at the end of the meal with the sweet course.
    a. True
    b. False

8. Which ice cream based treat was Jane Austen most likely to have eaten?
    a. Fried Ice Cream
    b. An Ice Cream Bombe
    c. Baked Alaska

9. When was ice cream considered 'in season'?
    a. summer
    b. winter

10. It usually took several hours to freeze ice cream to serving consistency in Jane Austen's day
    a. True
    b. False

How did you do? Find the answers under 'Q' for quiz!

CHAPTER 2

An A to Z of History of Georgian Ice Cream

Let's take an A to Z tour of ice cream in Jane Austen's world:

A is for Asparagus, a vegetable green;
one whose presence is not expected in ice cream.

B is for Biscuits and also for bread,
not on your plate, but in ice cream instead.

C is for Cheese. A treat for a mouse—
tell me do these sweets belong in your house?

D is for Drinks: Coffee and tea.
Turned into ice cream? Sounds quite good to me.

*E is for Emy, who wrote the first book
dedicated to ice cream—worth taking a look.*

*F is for Fanshawe who wrote the first way to
make icy cream;
it's also for the flavors of which we dream.*

*G is for Grown up- ice creams with a punch.
Not good for serving to children with lunch.*

*H is for Hokey; Hokey Pokey I mean.
What in the world has that to do with ice
cream?*

*I is for ice that's needed to freeze,
stored in the cold months to use as you please.*

*J is for jasmine, as in the flower.
For these ice cream flavors, we turn to the
bower.*

*K is for King. Charles I and II we are
told,
were ice cream lovers from days of old.*

*L is for Luxury—chocolate is one.
And if you ask me, it is the most fun.*

M is for Method by which we freeze,
something only recently done with great ease.

N is for NaCl. We know it as salt,
without which ice cream freezing would come
to a halt.

O is for Oyster, now add in some duck and
some meat—
surely those belong in ice cream-y treats.

P is for Pastry with ice cream inside.
What better place for a sweet treat to hide?

Q is for Quince and also for quiz;
check your answers below—you might be an
ice cream whiz.

R is for Rich. Who else could afford
the wonder of ice cream when they were
bored?

S is for Serving upon fine china plates,
in glasses to lick, ice cream they ate.

T is for Tea houses where ice cream was
bought.

At Gunter's a young lady might behave as
she ought.

U is for Unmolding the ices for all to behold.
Look at such beauty—it never gets old.

V is for Vanilla, a rare orchid fruit.
So popular now, there's no substitute.

W is for Wafers, crispy cookies to hold.
To put ice cream within them was really
quite bold.

X is for Cautions, the infirm beware:
Partake in that ice cream if only you dare.

Y is for Yolks of so many eggs.
After eating all these, you best stick to veg.

Z is for Zenith, where angels abound,
to bring you ice cream high above the ground.

A is for Asparagus

A is for Asparagus, a vegetable green;
one whose presence is not expected in ice
cream.

Innovation is Tradition

When it comes to ice cream, innovation is tradition. Ice cream lovers fall into two camps: those who love experimenting with innovative, exotic flavors and the purists, who remain loyal to vanilla. Wild experimentation is nothing new, though; it can be traced back to the earliest ice cream cooks.

While I'm not averse to experimenting and trying new things, at no time, ever, even in a toddler-induced, sleep deprived haze did I ever say to myself, "My family needs to eat more vegetables. I know I'll make them into ice cream." Nope, never went there. But I guess someone did. Cookbooks from the Georgian and Victorian eras chronicle some pretty ah—*interesting*—recipes for ice cream that are definitely worth mentioning here.

It is interesting to note that many of these vegetable ice creams have very little sugar. While we think of ice cream as a sweet, largely dessert dish, the French served frozen courses in the middle of the meal as an *intermezzo*, a palate cleanser to prepare the diner for the next big course. Sweets do not cleanse the palate well, so many early ice creams were not really sweet at all.

Although Mrs. Bennet (*Pride and Prejudice*) was known for setting an excellent table, the sort of meals she served were unlikely to have included a palate cleanser course. Those sorts of meals would have been much more likely at special events at homes like Mansfield Park or Kellynch Hall (*Persuasion*) where French cooks were more likely to have been employed.

I found a mention of asparagus ice cream in some of the articles I read, but could not actually turn up the cookbook it was supposed to be in, nor did any of the other cookbooks I have on hand have a recipe for it. So I thought I'd include a modern one (yes, I really did find one) that seems to be the closest to other historical recipes. I have not tried this, so try it at your own risk:

ASPARAGUS ICE CREAM

½ to 2 pounds asparagus, depending on how strong you want the flavor
6 large egg yolks
1/4 to 1/2 cup sugar
1 1/3 cups whole milk
1/4 cup heavy cream

Trim and cut asparagus. Cook in boiling salted water until tender; rinse under cold water. Reserve a few tips for garnish. (Ham slices and hollandaise sauce are other suggested garnishes. Just saying …) Puree asparagus and cream together in blender until smooth.

Mix egg yolks and sugar in a large bowl. In a saucepan, bring the milk a boil. Remove from heat. Slowly add to egg yolks and sugar, stirring well. Return mixture to sauce pan and heat gently until mixture coats the back of a spoon. Add asparagus puree and pour entire thing through a sieve.

Cool in the refrigerator, then churn according to your ice cream maker's directions.

If asparagus isn't to your liking, then how about channeling your inner Popeye for some spinach ice cream? From Marshall's (1888) famed book of ices. (Although this book was published well into the Victorian era, it contains many of the same recipes from French and Italian cookbooks published in the late eighteenth and early nineteenth centuries, so it is still representative of Georgian ice creams.)

ICED SPINACH A LA CREME (*Epinards Glacees ala Creme*).

Put 2 or 3 handfuls of spinach in cold water with salt, and a very tiny pinch of soda; let it come to the boil; strain off and press the water from it.

Boil half a pint of milk and stir it on to 4 yolks of eggs, and put it on the stove again to thicken—don't let it boil;

Add a little apple green to colour it, and to half a pint of the custard add a small dessert-spoonful of castor sugar and a pinch of salt. (Castor sugar is superfine sugar, finer than normal sugar, but not as fine as powdered sugar.)

Mix with the spinach, pass through the tammy, and freeze; *(A tammy is a sieve.)*

Add, when partly frozen, half a teacupful of whipped cream sweetened with a very slight dust of castor sugar.

Freeze dry and mould in a Neapolitan box in the cave for about 1½ hours; (A Neapolitan box was a rectangular ice cream mold. The cave is a double walled box where ice and salt were mixed between the two walls, dropping the temperatures inside of the box to freezing. Freeze dry meant to freeze solid.) (Marshall, 1888)

For the slightly less adventurous, this one actually sounds kinda good.

CUCUMBER CREAM ICE *(Creme de Concombres)*.

Peel and remove the seeds from the cucumber, and to 1 large-sized cucumber add 4 ounces of sugar and half a pint of water; cook till tender. Then pound and add to it a wine-glass of ginger brandy and a little green colouring and the juice of two lemons; pass through the tammy, and add this to 1 pint of sweetened cream or custard. Freeze and finish as usual. [Marshall, 1888]

(A fun little note, cucumber ice cream was often molded in cucumber or gherkin shaped molds before it was served. Asparagus molds were also very popular as were many fruit and vegetable shapes.

Portrait of Mrs. A. B. Marshall

But of course, I've saved the best for last! Truffle Ice Cream. I hate to disappoint though, when I refer to truffle, I'm not talking about the yummy chocolate kind, yeah, really!

In 1768, M. Emy wrote the first cookbook completely devoted to ice cream—*L'Art de bien faire les glaces d'office; ou Les vrais principes pour congeler tous les rafraichissemens.* Within the covers of this tome, he penned a recipe for truffle ice cream (truffles as in the fungi that grow underground.)

TRUFFLE ICE CREAM

There are several kinds of truffles: white, gray, black, and Piedmont truffles have a taste of garlic.

You need four ounces of truffles per pint of cream. Cook them in water with a little salt, then remove the skin and crush them and soak them in a little of the cream. When the mixture is smooth, put it in the cream base [above]. Thicken it over low heat. When it has a little consistency, remove from the heat and run it through a sieve, using a wooden spoon. Allow to cool (and freeze as per other ice creams). (Translation by David Young)

B is for biscuits and also for bread

B is for Biscuits and also for Bread,
not on your plate, but in ice cream instead.

The original cookies and cream

Cookies and cream is one of my very favorite ice cream flavors. It seems the idea originated with Emy in 1768. His book included recipes for a number of cookie ice creams in which the cookies, macaroons or biscuits, were crumbled up and added to the basic cream mixture. That mixture would be cooked down to reduce the volume, then strained like nearly all ice creams of the day, before freezing.

It seems silky smooth ice creams were the preference in the Georgian era, not the crunchy-chunky textures we enjoy today. Emy did suggest that just before serving, the ice cream be sprinkled with crunchy crumbs. I suppose it's not hard to make the leap from there to the cookie and cookie dough ice creams we enjoy today. (Quinzio, 2002)

BISCUIT ICE CREAM.

Break six eggs into a stew pan and beat them well with a wooden spoon; add one pint of cream, the rind of one lemon, two gills of syrup (*simple syrup, sugar and water*) and a little spice; boil it till you find it just thickens, stirring it all the time; crumble some Naples biscuits (*a biscuit flavored with rosewater*) and ratafia biscuits(*an almond-flavored cookie like a small macaroon*); pass them through a sieve with the other ingredients, and put it in your freezing pot. (Nutt, 1772)

Bread Ice Creams

Emy (1768) appears to have been the first (and possibly the only) one to suggest an ice cream flavored with rye bread. Admittedly, it's a little hard to wrap my head around what that would taste like. Maybe that's one reason I could not find the recipe repeated in any later cookbooks as so many others were.

GLACE DE CREME AU PAIN DE SEIGLE
(*Rye Bread Ice Cream*)

When the cream base is ready to come off

the heat, crumble rye bread (without the crust) into it and continue cooking to combine. With a wooden spoon, run through a sieve, letting some of the bread through. Allow to cool. Freeze. (Translation by David Young)

I envision this next one tasting rather like a piece of lightly sweet brown bread with sweetened butter on top. Not a bad image over all, really. This one might be worth trying.

BROWN BREAD CREAM ICES.

Take any quantity of cream, prepare it as we said before, boiling it alone with yolks of eggs. and the sugar, pass it through a sieve and put it in the sabotiere (*double pail ice cream maker*); when your cream begins to congeal (*freeze*), have crumbs of brown bread, which you have grated and sifted as fine as powder, put it in the sabotiere and continue to work your cream for congealing. You may also make this sort of cream with plain cream alone, without yolks of eggs, nor boiling, adding only a proper quantity of powdered (*extra fine, not powdered in the modern sense*) loaf sugar, and set it up to congeal, and when it begins to ice, then put your sifted crumbs of brown bread. But take care to have it so finely sifted, for it renders it infinitely more agreeable to the mouth. (Borella, 1772)

C is for Cheese

C is for Cheese. A treat for a mouse—
tell me do these sweets belong in your house?

Iced cheeses

Just to keep things interesting, iced cheese is a little confusing as it seems to refer to two distinctly different (wildly different some might say) concoctions. Some of these appear to be rich ice creams flavored with fruit, spice, even coffee or chocolate, and frozen into cheese-shaped molds and made to appear like different sorts of cheese, rather reminiscent of the cucumber and asparagus shaped ice creams mentioned earlier.

One can only imagine that Mr. Bennet (Pride and Prejudice), with his wry sense of humor, would have found these sorts of look-alikes quite amusing, especially if Mr. Collins confused one for actual cheese at the dining table. It isn't difficult to picture such a scene with Mrs. Bennet getting quite flustered and Elizabeth rolling her eyes. All this is conjecture though, as it is rather unlikely that Longbourn would have had an ice house to keep ice for the purpose of making such confusing confections.

These recipes are for ice cream molded into the shape of cheese.

ICED CREAM-CHEESE.

Boil a pint of good cream, then put half a pound of sugar to it, about a dozen of sweet almonds pounded, a little preserved orange-flowers, or orange-flower water, and rasped lemon-peel; boil together a few minutes; when you take it off the fire, add five yolks of eggs beat up, and stir it continually till they are well mixed with the cream; sift it in a sieve, and put it into the icing-pot: when it is pretty much iced, work it well to put it into cheese-moulds; ice it again, and serve as usual.—It is also done with coffee and chocolate in the same manner as the ices, only that each is thickened with four or five yolks of eggs, as directed in the first, and moulded like a cheese, which gives it the name. (Clermont, 1776)

Iced Cheese of any sort of Marmelade. *Fromage de Marmelade glaci*

They are made after the same manner; when the cream and eggs are well mixed, add a sufficient quantity of what marmalade you please to give it a proper taste of the fruit desired. (Clermont, 1776)

Don't start breathing a sigh of relief though, because, there were indeed another whole set of 'ice cheese' recipes that actually are flavored with—wait for it—actual cheese. Emy made a *glace de crème aux fromages* containing grated Parmesan and Gruyère (*see below*). Gilliers's *fromage de parmesan* mixed grated Parmesan with coriander, cinnamon, and cloves and froze it in a mold resembling a wedge of Parmesan cheese. Once it was unmolded, he recommended presenting it with a burnt sugar crust. (Quiznio, 2002) Honestly, I can't wrap my head around what Parmesan and cinnamon would taste like together, but maybe that's just me.

CHEESE ICE CREAM

Grate two ounces of Parmesan cheese and six ounces of Gruyere and mix with four egg yolks, a little cream and some sugar, then mix in the remaining cream. Thicken over low heat, stir often, making sure the Parmesan melts and both cheeses dissolve. Add sugar as necessary. Sieve and allow to cool. (Freeze) (Emy, 1768. Translation by David Young.)

PARMESAN ICE CREAM

Take six eggs, half a pint of syrup and a pint of cream put them into stewpan and boil them until it begins to thicken ; then rasp three ounces of parmesan cheese, mix and pass them through a sieve, and freeze it. (Nutt, 1789).

D is for Drinks: Coffee and tea

D is for Drinks: Coffee and tea.
Turned into ice cream? Sounds quite good to
me.

There were three luxury beverages a woman of Jane Austen's class might have expected to enjoy with some regularity: tea, coffee and chocolate. Not surprisingly, all of these found their way into the luxury confection: ice cream.

Tea

First up, let's put the teapot on ice!

TEA CREAM ICES

Make tea very strong in a tea-pot, have your cream ready mixt with the proper quantity of sugar and yolks of eggs, pass your cream through a sieve, pass likewise your tea over it, mix the whole well with a spoon, when that is done put it in the sabotiere (*double pail device used to freeze ice cream-*sThere were two primary forms in which ice cream could be served, molded and "rough." After the ice cream reached a soft frozen stage, it could be turned out into ice pails and brought to the dining room to be scooped into cups or glasses for service or it could be packed into molds. The molds would be frozen for several hours, then turned out on decorative platters, possibly colored with food safe dyes and accessorized according to the type of mold, then brought to the dining room.) and make it congeal (*freeze*) according to the usual method. (Borella, 1772)

ICED WATER GREEN OR BLACK TEA

Make a pint of strong fine green or black tea; put it in two pints of cream, with six ounces of sugar and five yolks; thicken it over the fire, strain, and when cold ice it. (a Lady, 1827) (Although Jane Austen's initial works were published under the same "a Lady" moniker, she did not write this, or any cookbooks that we know of.)

Coffee

When it came to coffee flavored ice creams, chefs really let their creativity run wild. The first of these recipes would produce a rich, caramel flavored coffee—if one managed not to burn the mixture. The second would be a much lighter almost café au lait kind of flavor.

COFFEE CREAM ICES

TAKE about a pint of coffee made with water, and rather strong, when settled, draw it clear (*strain out the coffee grounds*), and add half a pound of sugar, set it on the fire, and let it boil till your sugar is to the ninth degree; (*the caramel stage*) take it off from the fire and let it cool, after which, you make your cream as we said, with the yolks of eggs, and put your coffee in, then for boiling, sifting, and icing, proceed as usual. (Borella, 1772)

ICED WATER COFFEE.

Make eight cups of strong coffee, which will require half a pound; sweeten, and add to it fifteen cups of cream, with two or three yolks: thicken, cool, strain, and ice it. (a Lady, 1827)

Perhaps you'd like your coffee ice cream a little more luxurious. In that case, these recipes for iced coffee mousse and iced coffee soufflé might do. (Emy offered similar recipes in 1786, but Marshall's are very similar and a little easier to follow.)

COFFEE MOUSSE (MOUSSE AU CAFE).

12 yolks of eggs, 4 whites, 2 large tablespoonfuls of castor sugar(*superfine, but not powdered*), 2 large tablespoonfuls of strong coffee, also a little coffee colouring or es-

sence; whip over boiling water till warm, then take off and whip till cold, and add a teacupful of whipped cream; whip these well together. (*This adds up to an awful lot of whipping, all by hand!*) Put in a mould, and place in the cave (*a double walled metal box with ice and salt between the walls.*) to freeze for about 2½ hours. To turn out, dip the mould in cold water. Serve with dish-paper, or napkin on the dish. (Marshall, 1888)

*Emy's recipe would call for these recipes to be packed into molds and the molds sealed and plunged into a pail of ice and salt.

COFFEE SOUFFLE (SOUFFLE AU CAFE).

Take a soufflé dish and surround it inside with paper standing about 2 inches above the top, and put it into the charged cave to get cold. Take and whip over boiling water 12 raw yolks of eggs, 6 whites, 4 large tablespoonfuls of very strong coffee, 4 ounces of castor sugar (*superfine sugar*), until like a thick batter, then remove and continue the whipping on ice till the mixture is cold; to this quantity add 2 teacupfuls of whipped cream; pour this into the mould, letting it rise above the mould to near the top of the paper. Freeze in the cave for 2½ hours, and serve in the mould with napkin round or in silver soufflé dish. (Marshall, 1888)

If something more delicately flavored is your preference, fear not that can be accommodated with some white coffee ice creams. These feature a means of preparation and flavor that is not commonly seen today. In both of these offerings, whole coffee beans are boiled in cream, then removed. The cream picks up the coffee flavor, but remains very pale and delicate looking.

WHITE COFFEE CREAM ICES.

Prepare your cream as we have explained, take then a quarter of a pound of coffee in grain, which you roast as it were to make coffee with water; when roasted put it in a fine cloth, which you tye as a bag, and throw it quite hot in your cream; then set it on the fire keeping stirring till it offers to boil; take it off, pass it in a sieve, &c. &c. and proceed as usual for the rest. (Borella, 1772)

WHITE COFFEE CREAM ICE: (CRIME DE CAFE BLANCHE) VERY DELICATE

Take a quarter of a pound of fresh roasted Mocha coffee berries, and add them to a pint of cream or milk; let them stand on the stove for an hour, but do not let them boil; strain through tammy (*sieve*); sweeten with 3 ounces of sugar. Freeze and finish as for vanilla cream ice. (Marshall, 1888)

E is for Emy

E is for Emy, who wrote the first book
dedicated to ice cream—worth taking a look

By the second half of the eighteenth century, ices and ice creams had become so popular among Europe's ruling classes that M. Emy devoted an entire book to the subject: *L'Art de bien faire les glaces d'office ou, les Vrais Principes de congeler des tous les Rafraîchissemens (The Art of Making Ices or, The True Principles of Freezing All Sorts of Refreshments.* The 258 page tome, published in Paris in 1768, was aimed at food professionals, chemists and foodies, not home cooks. After all, only those who could afford a professional chef to cook for them could afford the ice and other ingredients for ice cream.

The book offered thorough and technical descriptions of the role and use of salt with ice to decrease the temperature of the freezing vessels and other similarly advanced techniques. He also provided detailed 'formulas' of various flavors and types of ice cream which he called a food fit for the gods. Previously, ice cream recipes were uncommon, scattered in general cookery books and largely unsatisfactory in terms of flavor and results. Emy's was the first work to deal with ice cream as a serious culinary discipline. (*Quinzio, 2009*)

His thoughtful approach to ice cream can be seen in these directions for making a cream base for ice cream.

CREAM BASE FOR ICE CREAMS

You need four egg yolks per pint of double cream, and about four ounces of sugar. Mix the yolks and a little sugar in a pan, then add the cream a little at a time. Heat gently to thicken the cream without boiling it. Stir it with a spoon of wood or silver, mixing it well or the bits of yolk will cling to the pot and form clots that prevent the cream from thickening properly, then when you freeze it, it will be grainy, and nothing you do will be able to fix it, and the result will be unhappy because the yolk which coagulated during cooking gets hard when frozen.

Stir, as I said, until the cream is quite thick, like a pulp. Do not let it boil. Allow an hour for stirring it, because it is on this first preparation that the results depend. Add more sugar if necessary.

Remove from heat--it will thicken further during cooling. Run through a sieve and allow to cool. Stir from time to time so that it does not form a skin on top and on the bottom a kind of clear milk, separating the parts. This is generally the best way to prepare all sorts of cooked creams; all that remains is to tell you how to add the different flavors.

I will refer to this article to avoid a number of repetitions which would be unnecessary; just pay attention to this article, to avoid all hazards that could happen to the cream. By following it point by point, you will be sure to succeed.

Other way

Whip the whites of four eggs until they are quite firm. Then mix in the four yolks and add a pint of cream little by little, mixing gently. Add sugar to taste. Thicken it and continue as in the previous article. This method of whipping the whites is popular with some people; I can't blame them, but I prefer the first version.

(Emy, 1768, translation by David Young)

Compared to Elizabeth Raffald's early recipe (1769), Emy was nothing if not thorough.

Modern eyes might consider many of his flavor suggestions more as rampant experimentation on what could be done with the medium of ice cream rather than dishes to actually at fancy meals. For bases, he froze custards, mousses, waters, wines; it seemed like anything he could put his hands on, he tried freezing. As to flavorings for his bases, he would try, it seemed, literally anything from ambergris (a waxy byproduct of a sperm whale's inability to digest squid beaks that's floated in the ocean, curing in the sun and salt—yum!) to verjus (the very sour juice of unripe grapes, crabapples or other sour fruits).

Seriously, he suggested ambergris ice cream:

AMBER ICE CREAM

To a pint of double cream, add two drops of essence of amber (*ambergris*) or a dash of powdered amber. Add powdered sugar to taste. (Emy, 1768, translation by David Young)

Clearly, nothing was off limits, including a few things that should have been, like truffles—the fungi not the chocolate variety Throughout his recipes, he cautioned his readers to constantly taste as they cooked and adjust ingredients accordingly. He even went so far as to recommend rinsing one's mouth between tastings. Clearly he was very serious about flavor. (Quinzio, 2002)

Interestingly enough, it seems that all we really know about M. Emy is found in the pages of his book. He was probably employed by an important family. Since he uses the title *officier*, he would probably have been the head of a department of professional ice cream makers. (Quinzio, 2009) The other details of his life, even what his first name was, appear to have been lost to history.

.

F is for Fanshawe and Flavor

*F is for Fanshawe who wrote the first way to
make icy cream;
it's also for the flavors of which we dream.*

The first known (as opposed to first published)
English recipe for true (dairy-based) ice cream
came long before Emy published his groundbreak-
ing book in 1768. The recipe was found
(unpublished) in the diary of Lady Anne Fanshawe,
an English memoirist and wife of Richard Fanshawe, Charles II's ambassador to the Spanish
court. (Ice cream wasn't the only recipe she recorded. Her memoires contain a very significant
collection of Stuart era recipes.)

The recipe was written around 1665 under the
name *icy cream.* (Kraft, 2014) You might notice
some interesting—and expensive—ingredients for
flavoring including orange blossom water, mace,
and ambergris. Honestly, between you and me, I

can't imagine what it must have tasted like.

Here's her recipe, complete with original seventeenth century grammar and spellings:

TO MAKE ICY CREAM

Take three pints of the best cream, boyle it with a blade of Mace, or else perfume it with orang flower water or Amber-Greece, sweeten the Cream, with sugar let it stand till it is quite cold, then put it into Boxes, ether of Silver or tinn then take, Ice chopped into small peeces and putt it into a tub and set the Boxes in the Ice covering them all over, and let them stand in the Ice two hours, and the Cream Will come to be Ice in the Boxes, then turne them out into a salvar with some of the same Seasoned Cream, so sarve it up at the Table.

It is interesting to note that as written, this recipe does not actually work. Unless you add salt to the ice, the cream will not freeze. This was probably just an oversight when writing it down, though, something I'm sure we've all done in the haste of trying to get a recipe jotted down so we don't forget it. Come to think of it, my kids have complained about that in a few recipes I've written down … but let's not go there just now.

Ann, Daughter of S'John Harrison of Balls
by Margaret Daughter of Thos Fanshaw Esq.
Wife to S'Rich. Fanshaw Bart. Amb. to Spain
Etched by CM Fanshawe

Early Ice Cream Flavors

In the early days of ice cream making, confectioners were uncertain about freezing techniques, worrying about how much ice they needed, how much salt to mix with the ice, and—perhaps most significantly—how keep the salt out of the ice cream. Beyond all that, they were concerned about storage and drainage, problems endemic to the days before refrigeration. Flavor, on the whole, seemed less important than freezing. (Quinzio, 2002)

By the late seventeen hundreds into the early eighteen hundreds, the freezing process was well enough established to really focus on flavors. A perusal of cookbooks from the eighteenth and early nineteenth century suggests that fruit flavors were probably among the most popular of ice creams. Elizabeth Raffald (1769) offered an early recipe, typical of future recipes (and one that later appeared in a number of other cookbooks thanks to lack of copyright protections, but that's another story…)

TO MAKE ICE-CREAM.

Pare and stone twelve ripe apricots, and scald them, beat them fine in a mortar, add to them six ounces of double-refined sugar, and a pint of scalding cream, and work it through a sieve; put it in a tin with a close (*tight*) cover, and set it in a tub of ice broken small, with four handfuls of salt mixed among the ice. When you see your cream grows thick round the edges of your tin, stir it well, and put it in again till it is quite thick; when the cream is all froze up, take it out of the tin, and put it into the mould you intend to turn it out of; put on the lid, and have another tub of salt and ice ready as before; put the mould in the middle, and lay the ice under and over it; let it stand four hours, and never turn it out till the moment you want it, then dip the mould in cold spring-water, and turn it into a plate. You may do any sort of fruit the same way. (Raffald, 1769)

And in fact, just about every sort of fruit, spice, flower and many vegetables did subsequently find their way into Georgian ice cream.

G is for Grown up

G is for Grown up- ice creams with a punch.
Not good for serving to children with lunch.

Nearly every meal in the Georgian era featured alcohol. Even breakfast often presented small beer at the table. While it did tend to keep the population perpetually buzzed, it also probably kept people alive considering the lack of safe drinking water. So it isn't very surprising to find a plethora of (heavily) alcoholic ice creams were served up, not only for dessert but for a between dance pick-me-up between dance sets at a ball.

Caroline Bingley would have likely had glasses of these sorts of ices passed around the ballroom between sets the Netherfield Ball (*Price and* Prejudice) to help the dancers cool off after their vigorous exercise. (From firsthand experiences, I can attest to the fact that Regency dancing then was very energetic.) After a couple of glasses of punch and a couple of ices, one would probably be well on her way to being in her cups. Kind of gives a new perspective on Lydia's behavior at the Netherfield ball, doesn't it?

WINE AND LIQUEUR ICES AND ICE CREAM
MUSCAT WINE ICE CREAM

To two bottles of excellent Frontignan or Lunel wine, add a half bottle of water or so, depending on the quality of the wine. The water will dilute the alcohol and make it easier to freeze. (If necessary, add more water.) Dissolve a half pound of sugar in it, to give it quality. Freeze. (Emy, 1768. Translation by David Young.)

NEGUS ICE

A bottle of port wine; half a nutmeg grated; one lemon rubbed, and scraped off sugar, with the juice of two; one pint of syrup, and freeze. (Cooke, 1824) [This recipe was recreated for the BBC2's documentary *'Pride and Prejudice: Having a Ball'*]

WHITE WINE CREAM ICE (*Crime au Vin blanc*).

Prepare a custard with 10 raw yolks of eggs, 1 pint of cream, and 4 ounces of sugar. When cool, add 3 glasses of white wine, 1 ditto pineapple syrup, and freeze. When frozen, mix in 6 ounces of finely cut preserved fruits of any kind you have, and mould if desired. (Marshall, 1888)

I rather like the serving suggestion on the following recipe.

AMERICAN SORBET (SORBET A I'AMERICAINE).

Make some imitation glasses (*glasses molded out of ice*), by freezing water in the proper tin moulds prepared for the purpose, and make a sorbet, flavouring it with Catawba wine or champagne. Serve the sorbet in the imitation glasses. These imitation cups or glasses can be made transparent, marble-like, or coloured. (Marshall, 1888)

ORANGE BLOSSOM RATAFIA ICE CREAM

To good orange blossom ratafia (*very sweet liqueur, often fruit based*), add a quart of water and a little orange blossom marmalade to increase the diluted flavor. Add sugar to taste. Freeze. (Emy, 1768. Translation by David Young.)

RUM SORBET (SORBET AU RHUM).

Prepare a lemon water ice, and when nearly frozen, flavour with 2 glasses of Jamaica rum to the pint of prepared ice. (Marshall, 1888)

Punch

Regency era punch was no child's party drink. It was very potent stuff. Typically it contained fruit juice and sugar, and a great deal of liquor, usually rum, but brandy, wine and champagne could also make an appearance according to the hostess' palate.

PUNCH WATER ICE.

Pare the rind very thin off one Seville orange, you are not to rasp it; put your parings into a bason, squeeze in two oranges and one lemon, put in two gills of syrup (*simple sugar syrup*) and half a pint of water, mix it and pass it (*through a sieve*); freeze it rich; when frozen and mixed well with your spoon, put as much rum in as you think will make it agreeable to the palate (*sounds like a dangerous sort of measurement to me...*) but when you put the rum in, take the freezing pot out of the ice while you mix it, which must be well done before you put it into the moulds. (Nutt, 1807)

ROMAN PUNCH (PUNCH A LA ROMAINE).

Boil 1 quart of water, and add to it 1 pound of sugar ; when quite boiling, pour it on to the peel of 3 lemons and the juice of 6 lemons; cover over till cold, then strain through the tammy (*sieve*), and freeze ; when partly frozen, add 2 glasses of Jamaica rum, and serve in sorbet cups or in glasses.

Another way.

Make 1 quart of lemon ice water; when cold, have the whites of 5 eggs whipped stiff, with a tiny pinch of salt, then add 4 ounces of castor sugar, and partly freeze the lemon ice, and then mix to it the whipped egg, and continue freezing in the machine till smooth ; when smooth, add 1 large wine-glassful of brandy and a half-pint of champagne ; continue to freeze, and serve in sorbet cups or in glasses. (Marshall, 1888)

Not exactly the sort of ice cream you'd serve at a kids' party is it?

H is for Hokey Pokey

H is for Hokey, Hokey Pokey I mean.
What in the world has that to do with ice
cream?

What does hokey pokey have to do with ice cream? Well, nothing during the Regency era, to be honest, but it was all so fascinating, I couldn't resist including it here. So, will you indulge a quick dive down the research rabbit hole?

I always thought of Hokey Pokey as this silly song/dance sort of thing we used to do at the roller skating rink when I was—well back in the dark ages anyway. Imagine my surprise, nay shock, to discover it had a far more interesting history!

As it turns out, Hokey Pokey has a long association with food. Food historians tell us that it traces back to Italian street vendors who sold inexpensive ice cream in the late nineteenth and early twentieth centuries. The term seems to come from an English interpretation of an Italian phrased used by the vendors: *O che poco*. Translated, it means "Oh, how little", a reference to the low price of their goods.

Hokey pokey venders generally peddled their wares on city streets and in places people went for recreation, like amusement parks, boardwalks, and resorts. They used small vehicles from hand carts, bicycle carts to goat-pulled wagons. Shop owners who sold ice cream were often contemptuous of their competition, using Hokey Pokey as a derogatory term for cheap goods and those who sold them.

What was Hokey Pokey?

Hokey pokeys were hefty slices cut from ice cream bricks. (Think about slices cut from the rectangular boxes of ice cream sold today.) In this case though, the bricks were generally about foot and a half long, a foot wide and two and a half to three inches deep. Not insubstantial by any means! They were usually layered with three different flavors of ice cream, and each crosswise slice would reveal all three, a bit like the Neapolitan ice cream we think of today, but the flavors were not nearly so predictable. Whole bricks were also available, sold to ice cream shops to be sliced and served, and to home consumers, who would have to rush home to serve them before the ice cream melted. (Quinzio, 2009)

HOKEY POKEY RECIPES

The recipes below offer some insight into why hokey pokey was so cheap. The confection included no cream, which was expensive. Instead they were thickened with corn starch and gelatin, far cheaper alternatives. It is interesting to note that neither recipe calls for any flavoring in particular, allowing for the use of whatever ingredients might be on hand, or be the cheapest at the time, to flavor the hokey pokey.

HOKEY POKEY

"Make a custard composed of 3 eggs, 1 quart of milk, 2 tablespoonfuls of corn starch, 6 ounces of pulverized sugar and sufficient of any desirable extract to flavor it. Bring the milk to the boil; mix the corn starch, 6 ounces of pulverized sugar and eggs; beat these smoothly together with a little cold milk and add it to the boiling milk; stir all till the mixture begins to thicken, then add and stir in the flavor. Now immediately remove it from the fire, and when it becomes cool stir it together and put it into your freezer and freeze till solid." (Stradley, 2017)

Another recipe "Dissolve three ounces of corn starch in one quart of milk, also soak two ounces of gelatin in the a little milk or water. Place three quarts of milk and one pound twelve ounces of sugar in a tin or porcelain-lined pan, set on the fire until boiling, then pour it over the dissolved starch and gelatin, set on the fire again and bring to a good boil, stirring constantly with the egg beater, then add one can of condensed milk, strain, cool and freeze. Flavor at will." (Stradley, 2017)

I is for ice

I is for ice that's needed to freeze,
stored in the cold months to use as you please.

Before the advent of artificial refrigeration, ice
was an essential ingredient to for chilled and frozen foods. Since it could not be made, it had to be
harvested during the winter and stored until used,
hence the development of the ice house.

The Ice House

The ice house was introduced to Britain in the
1600's when James I commissioned the first modern ice house in Greenwich Park in 1619. (Leslie,
2010) In 1682, Charles II had his own ice house
built in St. James Park. (Bourne, 2010) These
buildings maintained freezing temperatures even
through the summer months, with a combination
of ice packed tightly together, effective insulation
and thick walls.

Early ice houses were heavily insulated, subterranean chambers with north facing doors. Strategically planted trees might provide additional cooling shade for the ice house. Although designs varied, ice houses were usually conical or rounded at the bottom, with a drain to take away water (melted ice). Typically ice houses featured double-walled (and often double-doored) construction, with about nine inches between the two walls. Straw and boards might be placed between layers of ice for additional insulation.

Ice houses could be huge. The interior of Parlington Hall's ice house in Yorkshire measured sixteen feet in diameter by twenty feet deep. (Bourne, 2010) Although it seems primitive when compared to modern methods of refrigeration, properly built and maintained, ice houses could preserve ice for up to two years.

Ice houses were often built near a water source, like lakes, rivers or ponds, to facilitate the ice harvest. During the deepest part of winter, solid blocks of ice were cut from their sources and hauled by horses to the ice houses where they were carefully stacked, packed and insulated to remain frozen. Sometimes, in addition to the ice blocks (or instead, if ice was unavailable) snow was gathered, packed down tight in ice houses and water poured over it to help it to freeze solid. Occasionally, ships might bring ice chunks from glaciers or icebergs to port cities. These imported masses of ice would be carted to ice houses for preservation.

Ice house construction significantly increased in the seventeen hundreds. But only the wealthy could afford such luxuries. So ice houses were only found in or near great manor houses or the grand houses and villas of London and large cities.

Of Austen's families, the Elliots (*Persuasion*) and the Bertrams (*Mansfield Park*) were almost certain to have had ice houses on their estates, as were the families of Rosings Park and Pemberley (*Pride and Prejudice*). It is questionable whether the Wood-houses of Hartfield (*Emma*) would have had an ice house. The Bennets (*Pride and Prejudice*) and the Morlands (*Northanger Abbey*), almost certainly did not.

Large scale commercial ice trade did not begin until 1806, so until then, ice and ice cream remained the purview of the well-to-do. By the 1880's ice companies made ice relatively cheap and abundant.

J is for Jasmine—as in the flower

J is for Jasmine, as in the flower.
For these ice cream flavors, we turn to the
bower.

When we think of common ice cream flavors today, our minds usually go to vanilla. Back in the seventeenth and eighteenth century, vanilla (which is the fruit of the vanilla orchid—but you probably already knew that...) was pretty uncommon. Far more common flavors were floral ones, including jasmine, orange flower, violet, elder flowers and rose. (Quinzio, 2002) In fact, rose-water was one of the favorite flavorings for confections.

The flavors do sound quite lovely and ladylike. It is easy to picture fine ladies sitting down at a confectionary shop, or in a luxurious home to enjoy rose petal ice cream on a hot afternoon. Such a pretty picture, no?

Honestly though, I can't say I'm wild about

most flower flavors in my food. I've tried rose water beverages and syrups and my humble palate declares them to taste like perfume. And the times I've tried lavender flavored things, and, well, it tastes like soap to me. I do like jasmine and hibiscus teas, so there is that I suppose. Still, I'm not utterly convinced about floral ice creams. But here are a few recipes to let you make your own decisions about them.

At least they're not asparagus, right?

Flowers could be used to create water ices (sorbets) or ice creams, although 'a Lady' (below) observes that flower essences are more effectively derived from water than oil substances like cream.

Rose Water Ices and Ice Creams

ROSE SORBET
Put freshly gathered rose petals in a pot, add sugar water, and let infuse for twelve hours. Strain to remove the petals. If necessary, add water with a little carmine for a rose color. (Emy, 1768. Translation by David Young)

Marshall (1888) offers some more specific instructions for a similar confection.

ROSE WATER ICE (EAU DE ROSES).
Take half a pound of fresh-gathered rose

leaves, pour 1 pint of boiling water on them, with 4 ounces of sugar, and keep closely covered up ; then strain off and colour with a little liquid carmine, and freeze. (Marshall, 1888)

ICE CREAM OF ROSES.

Take two handsful of picked rose-leaves, and infuse them in a pint of rich boiling cream, and leave them covered for two or three hours; strain, beat the yolks of eight eggs, and mix with the cream; sweeten, stir it over a slow fire till it thickens, and, when cold, ice it.

It is to be observed that cream, or any oily substances, are ill calculated to extract essences, and that they would be better obtained by water, and added to the cream. (a Lady, 1827)

Orange Blossom Ices and Ice Creams

ORANGE BLOSSOM SORBET

If it is summer, clean beautiful, freshly gathered orange blossoms, put them in a pot and add tepid water in which sugar has been fully dissolved. Cover tightly, so that the flavor does not evaporate. Let it infuse for three or four hours, then strain it to remove the blossoms. If it has too strong a flavor of orange blossom, mix it with more sugar water to lighten the taste. Add lemon juice and a little water to lessen the sweetness and make it easier to freeze. (Emy, 1768. Translation by David Young)

Once again, Marshall steps in with a more exact version of a similar, though creamy, confection

ORANGE FLOWER WATER CREAM ICE (CRIME D LA FLEUR d'Oranger).

Blanch 4 ounces of sweet almonds and 6 bitter almonds (*these bitter almonds are not the poisonous, cyanide containing ones ones, but rather the seeds of stone fruits*); pound them in the mortar till quite smooth, then mix with a quarter of a pint of cream, 6 ounces of castor sugar, (*castor sugar was extra fine sugar, but not powdered*) and 7 raw yolks of eggs ; add, when this is mixed well, 1 pint of cream, and then thicken over the fire, and tammy(*put through a sieve*). When cool, add two wine glasses of orange flower water, and a few drops of essence of vanilla, and freeze. (Marshall, 1888)

Other Flowers used in Ices and Ice Creams

ICES OF VIOLETS, JESSAMIN, & ORANGE-FLOWERS.

Pound a handful of violets, and pour about a pint of hot water upon them; let them infuse about an hour, adding about half a pound of sugar; when it is properly dissolved, sift (*strain*) through a napkin.—The jessamin (*jasmine*) is done after the same manner: to make the liquid taste more of the different flowers, pour it several times from one pan into another before sifting; those different infusions are also mixed (*may also be mixed if desired*)with cream instead of water (Borella, 1772)

VIOLET SORBET

Clean beautiful, freshly gathered violet petals. Crush them and pass through a fine sieve. Boil them lightly with half sugar water and half plain water. Pass through a fine sieve again. (Emy, 1768. Translation by David Young)

MUSCADINE ICES WITH ELDERFLOWER

Take one ounce of eider flower, which you put in a sabotiere (*a double pail vessel, the earliest form of ice cream freezer*) pour upon it about, half a pint of boiling water, cover your sabotiere with its lid, thus let it draw about half an hour make then a composition precisely, as it were so make a plain lemon ice, and as directed in that article; to that composition add your infusion of elder flower, pass the whole through a sieve, and put it in the sabotiere to congeal (*thicken as the mixture freezes*) as we have explained. (Borella, 1772)

K is for King

K is for King. Charles I and II we are told,
were ice cream lovers from days of old.

History tells us that ice cream came to England by way of the royal tables, but there is some question as to exactly whose tables they were. Culinary mythology tells us that in the 1600s, King Charles I of England enjoyed "cream ice" so much that he paid his chef to keep the recipe a secret, so it would remain only a royal treat. (Upon, 2013) There is not a lot of evidence to support the claim, but it is not difficult to believe royalty might have wanted to keep the treat for themselves.

The first recorded appearance of ice cream in Britain, though, was at a feast given by Charles II. Elias Ashmole documents the menu for the feast for the Knights of the Garter held in St. George's Hall at Windsor Castle in 1671. At the dinner, 145 dishes were served during the first course alone. The Knights of the Garter were "offered 16 barrels of oysters, 2,150 poultry, 1,500 crayfish, 6,000 stalks of asparagus and 22 gallons of strawberries." (Day, 2012) One, just one single plate of ice cream was served at the same banquet, and that was at the sovereign's table.

Amidst the rest of the dishes, the knights probably never realized what they were missing! But since this was the same era in which Lady Ann Fanshawe penned her recipe for Icy Cream in her memoirs, someone outside of the royal party was definitely aware of the frozen confection.

L is for luxury—chocolate is one

L is for luxury—chocolate is one.
And if you ask me, it is the most fun.

Of the three luxury beverages of the Regency era, tea dominates the conversation, but coffee and chocolate were regularly enjoyed by many in the higher classes. Chocolate was typically served at breakfast, although specialty coffee and chocolate houses served it at all times during the day.

Recipes for chocolate treats in the form of ices, ice creams, custards and various pastries and tarts abounded in English cookery books. (But chocolate candies as we know them would not be around for some time yet.) Generally they began with a block of chocolate (usually used to make drinking chocolate) prepared from cocoa nibs.

Chocolate Tablets

It is easy to imagine these chocolate blocks

were like the chocolate we buy today, but it would not be accurate. They included a variety of ingredients we do not expect in anything but specialty chocolate today.

Hannah Glasse (1784) offered two recipes for preparing the nibs into chocolate tablets for use. The amount of spices added to both of these recipes is a bit mind boggling.

HOW TO MAKE CHOCOLATE.

Take six pounds of cocoa-nuts, one pound of anise-seeds, four ounces of long-pepper, one of cinnamon, a quarter of a pound of almonds, one pound of pistachios, as much achiote (*annatto, a red-orange condiment and food coloring*) as will make it the colour of brick, three grains of musk, and as much amber-grease (*ambergris from a sperm whale's digestive tract*), six pounds of loaf-sugar, one ounce of nutmegs, dry and beat them, and force them through a fine sieve; your almonds must be beat to a paste, and mixed with the other ingredients;

Then dip your sugar in orange-flower or rose-water, (*the sugar would be broken off a large loaf and would be a solid chunk able to be dipped in water*) and put it in a skillet, on a very gentle charcoal fire; then put in the spice, and stew it well together, then the musk and amber-grease, then put in the cocoa-nuts last of all then achiote, wetting it with the water the sugar was dipped in.

Stew all these very well together over a

hotter fire than before; then take it up, and put it into boxes, or what form you like and set it to dry in a warm place.

Another Way to make Chocolate.

Take six pounds of the best Spanish nuts (*cacao beans*), when parched, and cleaned, from the hulls, take three pounds of sugar, two ounces of the best cinnamon, beaten and sifted very fine; to every two pound of nuts put in three good vanelas, or more or less as you please; to every pound of nuts half a drachm of cardamom-seeds, very finely beaten and sieved. (Glasse, 1784)

Not surprisingly, most people preferred to purchase these tablets in a ready-made form. Manufacturers blended various flavorings into the chocolate tablets like Glasse recommended. Popular flavorings included mace, ambergris, aniseed, cloves, cardamom, bergamot, lemon peel, vanilla (at this time, vanilla was more considered a flavoring for chocolate than a standalone flavor. Click here for more about vanilla), cinnamon, nutmeg, orange-flower water, and rose water. During the Regency, the later five were the most popular.

Before you begin imagining these as luxury chocolate bars, they weren't. Without modern production machinery, the chocolate tablets were hard and gritty, not sweet, smooth and melty. A few people ate them straight as a type of candy, but most believed they would cause indigestion if eaten in that form. Not difficult to imagine that.

English Chocolate Ice Cream

These recipes from English cookbooks all begin with prepared chocolate tablets which were melted into water or cream. The spices included in the chocolate tablets could dramatically change the flavor of the ice cream from one batch to the next.

The first published English chocolate ice cream recipe features a startling lack of sugar:

TO MAKE CHOCOLATE-CREAM

Take a Quarter of a Pound of Chocolate, breaking it into a Quarter of a Pint of boiling Water. Mill it (beat it with a tool called a molinilla or chocolate mill, designed to raise a froth) and boil it, 'till all the Chocolate is dissolv'd. Then put to it a Pint of Cream and two Eggs well-beaten; let it boil, milling it all the while; when it is cold, mill it again, that it may go up with a Froth. (Eales, 1718)

This recipe from Borella illustrates the risk of making curds and whey out of your ice cream preparation if you don't pay close attention to it. Mmmm, chocolate curds and whey …

CHOCOLATE CREAM ICES.

Take chocolate, melt it over the fire in a small pan; when melted, you pour it into that where you are to make your cream; break into the same pan four yolks of eggs for every pint of cream you are to employ; mix the whole together, add some pounded loaf sugar to it, keeping stirring continually, then add your cream by little and little, in stirring and turning till the whole is mixed properly together.

Then set your pan over the fire, and keep stirring with a wooden spoon till you see your composition is willing to boil, when you are to take it off immediately; for from the moment you set your composition over the fire till that it offers to boil, it has a sufficient time to incorporate well and thicken sufficiently, without need of boiling; and should you let it boil, you would run the risk to make your cream turn into whey, on account of the yolks of eggs, which would do too much.

Take great care likewise your cream should be very fresh and sweet, for, otherwise, as soon as it would feel the warmth it would all turn into curds and whey; therefore, for all these considerations, you are to take care to stir it well and continually, from the moment you set it on the fire to that you take it off; after which you pour it into a sieve to pass it in a pan, then put it in the sabotiere to make it congeal (*freeze*) after the usual manner. (Borella, 1772)

Nutt offers a recipe that appears to be both sweet and without the cottage cheese risks.

CHOCOLATE ICE CREAM.

Take one ounce and a half of chocolate and warm it over the fire; take six eggs, one gill of syrup (*sugar and water syrup called simple syrup today*), and one pint of cream; put it over the fire till it begins to thicken; mix the chocolate in, pass it through a sieve and freeze it. (Nutt, 1807)

A French Approach

Apparently Emy, a French chef, took an entirely different approach to making his preferred chocolate cream. Instead of starting with a chocolate tablet, he began with roasted cocoa nibs that he steeped in hot cream and sugar like one would do with ground coffee beans. Both the following recipes would be light in color, and with a very different sort of chocolate flavor than the prior English recipes. It is also worth noting that these recipes lack the heavy spices that were typically found in English chocolate tablets.

CACAO ICE CREAM

For a pint of double cream, you need two ounces of roasted cacao. Beat two egg whites with powdered sugar until they make a clear paste. Add a pint of double cream and thicken over low heat, stirring, and avoiding boiling. Follow this article fully and don't let any of the cream stick to the pot. Taste it to see if there is enough sugar. When it is thick, separated from the watery part, take it off the fire. Break up the cacao (roasted like coffee, shell removed), mix with the hot cream, and cover tightly in a double boiler over hot water (no additional heat) for an hour and a half to two hours. Strain through silk and allow to cool. Freeze as per general method. (Emy, 1768. Translation by David Young)

This recipe by Emy resembles Glasse's second recipe for chocolate tablets with vanilla, cinnamon and ambergris. (What is does not resemble, though, is modern white chocolate.)

WHITE CHOCOLATE ICE CREAM
Using the recipe for Cacao Ice Cream [above], but before heating, add: half a dash of amber (ambergris) half a stick of vanilla, and two dashes of cinnamon. (Emy, 1768. Translation by David Young)

M is for Method

M is for Method by which we freeze,
something only recently done with great ease.

Freezing ice cream in the days before refrigeration

Early recipe books focused a great deal of attention to the freezing process. Eales's 1718 treatise, the first published English language ice cream recipe, is typical, suggesting you take any sort of cream you like (because clearly flavor really doesn't matter), then detailed how to freeze it.

TO ICE CREAM.

Take Tin Ice-Pots, fill them with any Sort of Cream you like, either plain or sweeten'd, or Fruit in it; shut your Pots very close (*close tightly*); to six Pots you must allow eighteen or twenty Pounds of Ice, breaking the Ice very small; there will be some great Pieces, which lay at the Bottom and Top: You must have a Pail, and lay some Straw at the Bottom; then lay in your Ice, and put in amongst it a Pound of Bay-Salt; set in your Pots of Cream, and lay Ice and Salt between every Pot, that they may not touch; but the Ice must lie round them on every Side; lay a good deal of Ice on the Top, cover the Pail with Straw, set it in a Cellar where no Sun or Light comes, it will be froze in four Hours, but it may stand longer; then take it out just as you use it; hold it in your Hand and it will slip out. (Eales, 1718)

Despite the fact that Mrs. Eales was the royal confectioner to Queen Anne, following her instructions produces a solid lump of iced cream, rather unlike anything we would eat today—or possibly be interested in eating given the lack of attention to flavor.

By the 1770's improved directions—separate from recipes for actual ice cream flavors—suggested stirring the mixture in a special vessel as it froze to maintain a pleasing texture.

THE WAY TO ICE ALL SORTS OF LIQUID COMPOSITIONS.

When your composition is put in the sabotiere (*freezing pot*) take some natural ice and put it in a mortar, when it is reduced into a powder strew over it two or three handfuls of salt; then take your pails, put some pounded ice in the bottom, and place your sabotiere in those pails which you fill up after with ice to bury the sabotiere in.

You must take care in the beginning to open your sabotiere in order not to let the sides freeze first, and on the contrary detach with a pewter spoon, all the flakes (*ice crystals*) which stick to the sides, in order to make it congeal (*freeze*) equally all over in the pot.

Then you must work them well as much as you are able, for they are so much the more mellow as they are well worked; and their delicacy depends entirely upon that. You must not wait till they are thoroughly iced to begin to work them, because they would become too hard and it is not possible to dissolve what is congealed in lumps or pieces.

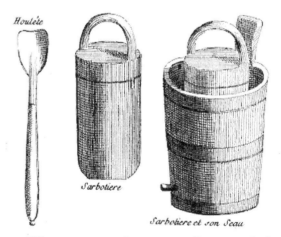

Houlette

Sarbotiere

Sarbotiere et son Seau

When you see they are well congealed you let them rest, taking care for this time there should be some which stick to the sides of the icing-pot: this will prevent them from melting and make them keep longer in a right degree of icing. (Borella, 1772)

The sabotiere Borella mentions is a piece of equipment dedicated to making ice cream. It consists of a pewter freezing pot with a tight fitting lid to contain the cream or water to be iced, an ice spaddle or houlette to scrape down the freezing pot, and a large bucket, often of wood, to hold the water and ice mixture. Similar to another luxury food, chocolate, ice cream could certainly be made without the specialty items by repurposing standard kitchen items for the task, but in wealthy households, the specialized tools would be a must. (Image from Emy, 1768)

So, if the Bennets (Pride and Prejudice) were able to obtain the ice to make ice cream, they would likely use a make shift a sabotiere with items already in their kitchen, probably using a standard pail and a cooking pot. In all likelihood, they would end up with some salt water splashing into the ice cream since their freezing pot would probably lack a tight fitting lid. But hey, that could have been the origin of salted caramel ice cream, right?

By the nineteenth century, cookbooks began to describe the ideal specifications for sabotieres.

OBSERVATIONS ON ICE CREAM.

… A freezer should be twelve or fourteen inches deep, and eight or ten wide. This facilitates the operation very much, by giving a larger surface for the ice to form, which it always does on the sides of the vessel; a silver spoon, with a long handle, should be provided for scraping the ice from the sides, as soon as formed, and when the whole is congealed, pack it in moulds (which must be placed with care, lest they should not be upright,) in ice and salt till sufficiently hard to retain the shape--they should not be turned out till the moment they are to be served.

The freezing tub must be wide enough to leave a margin of four or five inches all around the freezer when placed in the middle, which must be filled up with small lumps of ice mixed with salt--a larger tub would waste the ice. The freezer must be kept constantly in motion during the process, and ought to be made of pewter, which is less liable than tin to be worn in holes and spoil the cream by admitting the salt water. (Randolph, 1824)

Crank Turned Ice Cream Makers

The familiar modern crank turned version of an ice cream freezer did not appear until the Victorian era. Nancy Johnson patented the first model in 1843. William Young bought the patent and marked the machine as the Johnson Patent Ice-Cream Freezer.

A.B. Marshall of the Marshall Cookery School

of Mortimer Street, London, and author of the *Book of Ices* often quoted here, also sold a patent ice cream freezer which she claimed would freeze a pint of ice cream in five minutes. That is faster than most modern home use ice cream makers. Sounds unbelievable, but food historian Ivan Day (*Asparagus Ices*, 2004) tested the claim and found it true.

56

BY ROYAL LETTERS PATENT.

MARSHALL'S PATENT FREEZER.

Complete View.

IS PRAISED BY ALL WHO KNOW IT FOR

CHEAPNESS in first cost.   CLEANLINESS in working.
ECONOMY in use.   SIMPLICITY in construction.
RAPIDITY in Freezing.

NO PACKING NECESSARY.   NO SPATULA NECESSARY.

Smooth and delicious Ice produced in 3 minutes.

Sizes—No. 1, to freeze any quantity up to one qt., £1 5 0.
No. 2, for two qts., £1 15 0.   No. 3, for four qts., £3 0 0.   No. 4,
for six qts., £4 0 0.   Larger sizes to order.

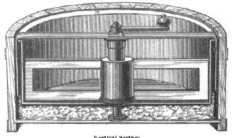

Vertical Section.

N is for NaCl

N is for NaCl. We know it as salt,
without which ice cream freezing would come
to a halt.

For all the fancy equipment and recipes for ice cream, there is one single ingredient that makes every Regency era ice cream possible—and it's not sugar. Nope, not that sugar isn't important, but the crucial ingredient is salt.

Effect of Salt (and Sugar) on Freezing

What makes salt so critical? It is not as though it is actually an ingredient in the ice cream mixture itself. In this case it isn't about the taste, it is about the chemistry, the chemistry of freezing.

If you were to simply take a container of cream, sugar and flavoring and plunge it into a bucket of ice or even ice water, how long would it take for it to freeze into ice cream? (Cue Jeopardy theme music.) Times up, and the answer is … never. You might get a nice cold batch of tasty cream, but what you would not get is ice cream. This was the problem with Fanshawe's Icy Cream recipe that we mentioned earlier.

But why?

Ice alone will not get the cream solution cold enough to freeze. The addition of sugar to the cream (or alcohol in some cases) lowers the freezing temperature of the solution to something on the order of 20F (-6.7C), significantly below the freezing point of water.

So then, if salt melts ice, how does it help the situation?

Adding salt to ice creates an endothermic reaction—a fancy way of saying a reaction that makes things cold instead of hot. Salt lowers the freezing point of water, causing it to draw heat from its surroundings to allow it to transform back into its liquid state, in other words, melt. This produces a brine with a temperature of about 17F (-8.3C). Even better, this liquid brine is ideal to transfer its cold to a metal freezing pot of ice cream.

Of course this salty solution creates a new problem: keeping the salt brine solution out of the ice cream! The lid of the freezing pot had to fit very tightly to keep the salt water out. The entire affair needed to be washed thoroughly after use to keep the corrosive effects of the salt at bay. Ice cream molds presented an entirely different challenge, especially hinged ones with seams. In that case, a variety of substances were used to act as a barrier against the salt water, including butter, lard and wax. After use, the molds, too, had to be washed very carefully to keep corrosion at bay. That was one advantage the porcelain ice pails had over molds, the salt did not damage porcelain surface, so it was an ideal material to keep the brine and the ice cream separate. Which is of course why it fell out of favor in preference to ice cream molds which always ran the risk of leaking salt into the ice cream.

Silly people, preferring pretty over practical!

So how did Regency era folks figure out how to used salt to make things freeze? Interestingly, endothermic chemical reactions were known and used in food preparations nearly five hundred years ago. In 1558, Italian scholar Giambattista della Porta published Natural Magick. In his book, he recommended people mix saltpeter (potassium nitrate) and ice to create a cooling solution, then dip a vial of watered wine into the mixture, until it "congealed" to make a kind of wine slush. (Georgian era cookbook writers would use this same term to describe freezing ice cream several hundred years later.) The secret of icing drinks slowly spread across Europe until, a hundred years or so later, ice cream emerged as a royal delicacy. (Inglis-Arkell, 2015)

The saltpeter trick was one that many upper class butlers knew as a means to chill wine for a dinner party in an "emergency" situation when there was no ice available. I can easily imagine a butler at Pemberley (Pride and Prejudice) performing such a feat..

O is for oyster

O is for oyster, now add in some duck and
some meat—
surely those belong in ice cream-y treats.

Well, if we're going to serve vegetable and cheese ice creams, it isn't much of a hop from there to meat, right? In for a penny, in for a pound as they say—so here we go…

Up first, oyster ice cream. This one comes from *The Virginia Housewife* (1824), a relative of Thomas Jefferson.

OYSTER CREAM.

Make a rich soup, (see directions for oyster soup,) strain it from the oysters, and freeze it.

Oyster Soup.

Wash and drain two quarts of oysters, put them on with three quarts of water, three onions chopped up, two or three slices of lean ham, pepper and salt; boil it till reduced one-half, strain it through a sieve, return the liquid into the pot, put in one quart of fresh oysters, boil it till they are sufficiently done, and thicken the soup with four spoonsful of flour, two gills of rich cream, and the yelks of six new laid eggs beaten well; boil it a few minutes after the thickening is put in. Take care that it does not curdle, and that the flour is not in lumps; serve it up with the last oysters that were put in. If the flavour of thyme be agreeable, you may put in a little, but take care that it does not boil in it long enough to discolour the soup. (Randolph, 1824)

Before you react too strongly to this one, let's leap ahead to modern day. Oyster ice cream was featured on the 1999 American debut of Iron Chef (a cooking competition show that originated in Japan.) Since then, Iron Chef has also featured ice creams flavored with parmesan cheese, trout, black truffle, scallops and pork to name just a few. Just something else that goes to show the more things change, the more they stay the same. Kind of makes the following recipes for ham, foie gras, and whiting(fish) ice creams look pretty tame.

LITTLE CREAMS OF HAM ICED. (*Petites Cremes de Jambon Glacees.*)

Whip half a pint of cream till quite stiff, then mix with it a quarter of a pint of liquid aspic jelly and a few drops of carmine to make it a pale salmon colour, add a dust of cayenne, and five ounces of lean cooked ham that is cut up in very little dice shapes; stir all together over ice until it begins to set, then put it in a Neapolitan ice mould and place this in the ice cave for about one and a half hours; when sufficiently iced dip the mould in cold water, remove the covers ,and turn the ham cream on to a clean cloth, cut it in slices crossways, and dish them up on a dish-paper in a round over-lapping one another; garnish the centre with a bunch of picked mustard and cress or any nice salad, and decorate the slices with ham butter by means of bag and fancy pipe. (Marshall, 1890)

ICED CREAM WITH FOIE GRAS A LA CANETON. (*Creme glacee au Foie Gras a la Caneton.*)

Take one and a half pints of cream and season it with a pinch of cayenne pepper and a little salt; mix with it three quarters of a pint of liquid aspic jelly and freeze in the freezing machine until the mixture is setting, then line the duck mould with it, colouring a small portion with a little of Marshall's apricot yellow to represent the beak of the bird.

When the mould is lined, fill up the centre with the contents of a jar or tin of pate de foie gras from which the fat has been removed, then close up the mould and put it into the charged ice cave or in a mixture of ice and salt to freeze for about one hour; if placed in ice and salt the joints of the mould should be lined with dripping to prevent the brine entering.

When frozen dip the mould into cold water and turn out the duck on to a bed of chopped aspic jelly and garnish it round with little eggs, made by putting a portion of the cream and foie gras in small egg moulds and freezing them similarly to the duck, and little blocks of cut jelly and sprigs of picked chervil. If you have glass eyes for the duck they give it a finished appearance. Serve for an entree or second course dish, or for any cold collation. The same mould may be used for a large variety of different dishes. (Marshall, 1890)

SOUFFLES OF CURRY A LA RIPON
(Petits Souffles de Karl a la Ripon).

Fry in about 2 ounces of fresh butter, 2 onions sliced, 2 sour apples, sprig of thyme, 2 bay leaves, sprig of parsley, about 1 ounce of cocoanut and a cup of almonds blanched; to this add a raw or cooked sole or whiting. Fry all until a good golden colour, then add half a teaspoonful of curry powder, half a teaspoonful of curry paste, half a teaspoonful of tamarinds, little salt, and juice of 1. lemon; cover then with milk and cook till tender, add a little saffron yellow to colour. Take the meat from the fish-bone and pound, and pass through a tammy cloth ; add a quarter of a pint of this puree to a good quarter of a pint of whipped aspic and half a pint of whipped cream; whip well together. Freeze in cases in cave for 1½ hours. When serving, garnish with prawns. (Marshall, 1888)

(Just an interesting note: Marshall seems to hold the patent for the Marshalls Ice Cave used in making all her recipes, which may just explain a few of the recipes above. It might give you a little comfort to know that these were not meant as desserts. She published these mid-meal sorbets in both of her cookbooks proclaiming they had an acknowledged place in serving a *first-class dinner*. Both her books were published in the Victorian era, well out of Jane Austen's day, but they are just so interesting I had to include them.)

P is for Pastry with ice cream inside

P is for pastry with ice cream inside.
What better place for a sweet treat to hide?

"Fried" ice cream and fancy Baked Alaskas appear on modern menus often enough that we are lulled into thinking it is a relatively recent addition to the culinary world. But alas, that assumption would be wrong.

While we have no actual evidence in her letters or other writings to suggest it, in terms of just the timeline, it is possible Jane Austen could have eaten frozen cream in a hot edible shell:

"Washington, February 10, 1802. 'On Tuesday I wrote that I was going to dine with the President [Jefferson]. The party was easy and sociable, as all these parties are. Among other things ice-creams were produced in the form of balls of the *frozen* material inclosed in covers of *warm pastry*, exhibiting a curious contrast, as if the *ice* had just been taken from the oven.'"—Dr. Mitchill's Letters From Washington: 1801-1813," *Harper's New Monthly Magazine*, April 1879 (p. 744) (in Olver, 2004)

Granted, she did not dine with presidents, but her brother was wealthy, there is just the barest possibility that he might have hired a cook who had heard of such a thing and dared try it at Chawton. Yeah, it's a stretch I know. But I'm sure she would have enjoyed the novelty of such a thing.

As for a Baked Alaska, it was definitely not to be found in Austen's day. However, it was around, in a cook book published in London, to see the end of the Georgian era under the name of Hot Cream Ice.

HOT CREAM ICE.

Make ratafia (an almond-flavored cookie like a small macaroon) or biscuit cream, as directed; freeze it, and put in a shape (mold), to get very hard ; when turned out put it on a thick board ; cover it over with a mixture made of eight whites of eggs beat up stiff, and mixed with twelve spoonsful of sifted sugar ; put it in a hot oven three minutes till the outward coat gets brown; put it on a dish and serve it immediately. (Cook, 1824)

Other similar recipes appeared later with names like Omelete Norvegienne, Omelete en Surprise. Why call it "omelete?" Probably because the ice cream was covered in eggs and finished in an oven like French dessert omelets were. (Olver, 2004)

(In case you're like me and wonder how either of these works, it's all in the physics. Apparently neither pastry dough nor whipped egg whites are good conductors of heat. So while they are browning up in the oven, the ice cream stays insulated inside. So now you know!)

.

Q is for Quince and also for Quiz

Q is for Quince and also for quiz;
check your answers below—you might be an
ice cream whiz.

Quinces were considered an exotic fruit during the Regency era, imported from Asia. Eaten in great quantities, the seeds can potentially produce hydrogen cyanide gas in the stomach. Sounds healthy, right? Seems to go right along with arsenic contained in wall papers, but that's another book.

QUINCE CREAM ICE *(Crime, de Coings).*
Take a teacupful of quince jam, and add to it the juice of 2 oranges and of half a lemon, 1 1/2 pints of cream or custard (unsweetened), a little apricot yellow to colour, 2 tablespoonfuls of pine-apple syrup. Pass through

the tammy (sieve), and freeze. (Marshall, 1888)

Ice Cream IQ Answers:
1.c 2.b. 3.a 4.b 5.b 6.a 7.b 8.a 9.a 10.b

.

R is for Rich

*R is for Rich. Who else could afford
the wonder of ice cream when they were
bored?*

Throughout Jane Austen's life, ice cream was only accessible at the homes of the wealthy or as a treat purchased from a confectioner or tea house that sold it. The producers of the 1995 *Persuasion* movie adaptation used ice and the anticipated lack of it as a way to illustrate the financial problems of the Elliot family. Although it was not a scene that Austen wrote herself, it is one she would have understood very clearly. In fact, she alluded to it in *Emma*, when describing Mrs. Elton's entrance into Highbury society, "She was a little shocked at the want of two drawing rooms, at the poor attempt at rout-cakes, and there being no ice in the Highbury card-parties." Maple Grove had clearly taught her to expect more than Highbury could provide.

Not only was ice expensive, but many of the ingredients to make ice cream were also very dear.

Among those, the salt required to freeze it, the cream that often formed its base and exotic spices imported for flavorings. Saffron, clove and coriander-seed were just a few of the flavors that made an appearance on Georgian tables and reflected the wealthy refined tastes that partook in ice cream.

Today, saffron is considered the most expensive spice. (Vanilla is the second most expensive— seriously it is!) It was likely equally dear in Emy's day (1768) when he penned this recipe.

SAFFRON ICE CREAM

Before heating the cream base, add a little saffron. (Then proceed as otherwise directed to freeze the mixture.)

CINNAMON ICE.

Infuse a proper quantity of cinnamon about an hour in hot water, and boil it a moment, add half a pound of fine sugar to a pint of water; sift it through a sieve, and finish as other (ice creams.) (Clermont, 1776)

This recipe is more of a 'water ice' than an ice cream. The recipe below would produce a much richer result.

CINNAMON CREAM ICE (CRIME DE CANNELLE).

Put 1 pint of milk or cream to boil with a fingerlength of cinnamon, 1 bay leaf, and the peel of half a lemon; when well flavoured, mix it into 8 raw yolks of eggs and 4 ounces of castor sugar (*extra fine sugar*); thicken over the fire. Add a little apricot yellow; tammy (*sieve*), and finish as for other ices. (Marshall, 1888)

The following two sound like they might be very good with a holiday dinner.

GINGER ICE CREAM.

Take four ounces of ginger preserved, pound it and put it into a bason, with two gills of syrup(*simple sugar syrup*), a lemon squeezed, and one pint of cream; then freeze it. (Nutt, 1807)

CLOVE ICE CREAM

Pound coarsely two ounces of the best cloves in a mortar; add to it four ounces of white sugar; boil two quarts of milk and throw in the cloves and sugar mixed, let it simmer for ten minutes tightly covered; then add one quart of cream, with half a pound of white sugar, let these only scald; then press all through a hair sieve, and freeze it; a nice after dinner ice. (Goodfellow, 1865)

ICES OF CORIANDER-SEED, ANISE-SEED, AND JUNIPER-BERRIES.

Bruise an ounce of coriander-seed, infuse them about an hour in a pint of warm water, with half a pound of sugar, and sift through a napkin: anise-seeds are done the same, and taste must direct, when the water has got a sufficient flavour of the different infusions: that of juniper-berries is done also by infusion, or by boiling a moment about a handful of the berries, with a pint of water, half a pound of sugar, and a bit of cinnamon; sift as usual, either through a fine sieve, or a thin napkin or cloth. (Clermont, 1776)

COOLING WATERS OF FENNEL, AND OF CHERVIL.

These are done simply, by steeping some of either in hot water till it has the taste of the herbs sufficiently; add what quantity of sugar you think proper, and keep it in a cool place a good while before using: the same is done with any other kind of herbs, and in general with all sorts of fruit used in confectionary; also with the syrups of liquid preserves, mixing some of the liquor with water and sugar just sufficient to make it palatable: it may be either iced or not. (Clermont, 1776)

Technically, tamarind is a fruit, but since it is used more like a spice, it seemed to fit here well.

TAMARIND CREAM ICE.

Take half a pound of tamarinds, three spoonsful of syrup; warm it together, and add one pint and a half of cream; rub it through a sieve and freeze. (Cooke, 1824)

TAMARIND WATER ICE.

Take one pound of tamarinds, a quarter of a pint of syrup a pint and a half of water; heat it together; rub through a sieve, and freeze. (Cooke, 1824) *This recipe was reproduced and used in BBC2's documentary: *Pride and Prejudice: Having a Ball.*

S is for Serving

S is for Serving upon fine china plates,
in glasses to lick, ice cream they ate.

Since ice cream was (during Austen's day) a luxury only the wealthy could enjoy at home, it is hardly surprising that there was a ready market for all manner of accessories with which to properly eat the delicacy.

There were two primary forms in which ice cream could be served, molded and "rough." After the ice cream reached a soft frozen stage, it could be turned out into ice pails and brought to the dining room to be scooped into cups or glasses for service or it could be packed into molds. The molds would be frozen for several hours, then turned out on decorative platters, possibly colored with food safe dyes and accessorized according to the type of mold, then brought to the dining room.

Ice Pails

If served rough, ice cream would be brought to the table in a special ice pail, a *seau à glace*. The design, first available in the 1720's, featured three pieces, an outer pail which held ice and probably salt, an inner bowl that held the ice cream, and a lid upon which you would pile more ice and salt. Modern experiments have shown that a pail like this one could keep ice cream frozen for up to four hours. (Day, 2004)

Porcelain was the preferred material for these pails. The salt solution in the upper and lower parts of the vessel would damage other materials, allowing it to find its way into the inner liner and contaminate the ice cream.

Ice cream pails often had feet to hold them above the tablecloth. Earlier models without the feet would eventually soak the tablecloth with condensation and possibly freeze to it as well. Thus, early ice cream pails were place on napkins or plates. Ice cream pails were rarely made after 1830 due to the increased popularity of molded ice creams. (Day, 2004)

Ice Cream cups and spoons

Not surprisingly, special dishes and utensils developed for eating ice cream as well.

Ice cream served rough required cups or glasses which had distinctly different shapes than cups for coffee, tea or chocolate. Most noticeably ice cream cups had feet, usually hollow. Some sources suggest that this was because it made it better for servants to handle (serve) them. Hollow feet would also insulate the bottom of the cup and protect them from condensation which would make them adhere to a tablecloth, much like the footed ice cream pails. (Illustration from Emy, 1768)

Most ice cream cups also sported distinct, scrolled handles which would keep the diner's fingers away from the body of the cup, protecting them from the cold and the ice cream from the heat of their hands. Finally, the cups were narrower at the bottom than at the top, like ice houses, funneling the melted ice cream to the bottom of the cup and away from the rest of the frozen mass. Narrow and sometimes long spoons were designed to allow the ice cream at the bottom of the cup to be reached easily.

Gobelets à glace

These special *tasse glace* were not among the common cups manufactured for common sets. One more way in which ice cream was a food for the wealthy.

For molded ice creams, a slicer was provided to cut into the mold and special plates used to serve the ice cream. A second form of ice cream spoon, wider and more spade-shaped appeared to be used with sliced ice cream on plates. This shape would allow eaters to scoop up the tasty bits of melted ice cream. By the Victorian era, special spork-like ice cream forks developed to help diners break off bits of hard frozen ice cream with the sharp tines then scoop them up with the spoon-like bowl.

Penny Lick Glasses

After the rise of the ice trade during the Victorian era, ice cream became more available to the masses through street vendors. Another kind of ice cream serving vessel came on the scene, the penny lick glass.

These shallow glasses were topped with ice cream for a customer to lick directly from the glass and return to the vendor. If one was lucky, the glasses were washed and then filled for the next customer. Needless to say, sanitation was perpetually a problem. Vendors often could not wash dishes fast enough to keep up with demand. It isn't difficult to imagine the glass simply being wiped out and used again. Penny lick glasses were banned in London in 1899 due to health concerns, increasing the popularity of ice cream cones..

T is for Tea Houses

T is for Tea houses where ice cream was
bought.
At Gunter's a young lady might behave as
she ought.

The wealthy and privileged of England and Europe enjoyed ices and ice creams in their homes during the late seventeenth century. Lack of access to ice and ice houses kept the less elite from being able to prepare the delicacy themselves, but it did not stop them from wishing they could. Enterprising French and Italian confectioners recognized the potential market. They started setting up shops at home and abroad to a provide iced treats to a less rarified (than peers and royalty), but still able to pay, clientele

Jane Austen's characters (and possibly even Jane herself) did visit shops run by pastry cooks where they could enjoy ice and ice cream. In Austen's juvenilia novel *The Beautifull Cassandra*, the heroine "… then proceeded to a Pastry-cook's, where she devoured six ices, refused to pay for them, knocked down the Pastry Cook & walked away." Clearly not the normal behavior for an Austen heroine, but it was meant as a parody after all.

Austen's later heroines demonstrated far better manners in taking their ices. From Northanger Abbey:

Such was the information of the first five minutes; the second unfolded thus much in detail — that they had driven directly to the York Hotel, ate some soup, and bespoke an early dinner, walked down to the pump-room, tasted the water, and laid out some shillings in purses and spars; thence adjoined to eat ice at a pastry-cook's, and hurrying back to the hotel, swallowed their dinner in haste, to prevent being in the dark; and then had a delightful drive back, only the moon was not up, and it rained a little, and Mr Morland's horse was so tired he could hardly get it along.

Paris

Cafe Procope 1675

Italian immigrant Francesco Procopio dei Coletti proved quite the businessman and entrepreneur. He started working for a coffee-house in 1672 and before long he opened his own coffeehouse. Not long afterwards, he ran a chain of coffeehouses throughout central Europe. He opened *Café Procope* in Paris in 1675. There he sold Viennese-style ices and custard-rich ice creams to the largely elite audience who could afford them. Coffee houses in Italy followed the Paris model, and gelato became widely popular and others began following his example. (Mariani, 1998)

London

The Pot and Pineapple 1757

In 1757, Italian pastry chef Domenico Negri opened a confectionary shop at the sign of *The Pot and Pineapple* in Berkeley Square which would become one of the best known confectionary

establishments in London history. For twenty years, the shop flourished, selling not only ices and ice creams, but baked goods as well.

The shop employed famous apprentices like Frederic Nutt, William Jarrin, and William Jeanes. Two of these apprentices published their own recipe books featuring large sections on ice cream. (Sanborn, 2013). (Nutt's *The Complete Confectioner* is quoted here extensively.)

In 1777, Negri took a business partner, James

Gunter who would take the business into the next century.

Gunter's Tea House 1799

In 1799, James Gunter had become *The Pot and Pineapple's* sole proprietor and changed the name to *Gunter's Tea Shop*. The Berkeley Square location was uniquely situated to appeal to the upper crust.

Over the next decades, Gunter's had become a favorite place of the Beau Monde to stop for a cool ice during carriage rides. A practice formed that ladies would eat their ices in their carriages across the street from the shop, while their escorts leaned against nearby railings and waiters carried wares back and forth across the road.

Though etiquette insisted that it was inappropriate for a lady to be seen alone with a gentleman at a place of refreshment, Gunter's became the exception to the rule. A lady could be seen there without damage to her reputation.

On top of its status as a spot to see and be seen, Gunter's was also known for its catering and beautifully decorated tiered cakes. In 1811, the Duchess of Bedford's and Mrs. Calvert's ball suppers featured Gunter's confectionery.

Unfortunately no Regency period images of Gunter's exist today, so we can only imagine what it may have looked like.

Other tea houses 1815

Though it was perhaps the best known, Gunter's was, by far, not the only place one could enjoy ice cream in Regency London. *The Epicure's Almanack* from 1815, a guide to good eating establishments, lists a number of venues which served "abundant varieties of delicious ice cream."

- *Angel's and Sons Pastry Shop*: At the south side of Gracechurch Street and corner of Cornhill, one could find abundant varieties of delicious confectionery, ice cream and fruit.
- *Rich's Pasty Shop:* On the south side of Ludgate St, adjoining the Albio Fire office. Here, soups, savory patties and jellies with ices in season and pastry of every kind were constantly supplied in the highest and most inviting condition
- *Farrance's:* On the corner of Ave Maria Lane and Ludgate St. This old established pastry shop served soups, savory patties, ices in great variety and confectionery.
- *Parmentier:* Three doors from Duke St. on the north side of Edward St.: The confectioner to the Prince Regent and Dukes of York and Kent.
- *George's Pastry-shop:* No. 6 Blandford Street. The shop produced delicious ices throughout the season.
- *Tupp's pastry shop*: Just to the east of the Stratford Hotel. The shop has long enjoyed the well-earned reputation of vending excellent soups, savory patties and pies, with pastry and ices in the most abundant varie-

ty.
- *The Blenheim Coffee House:* On the corner of Blenheim Street and New Bond Street. Jellies, ices and liqueurs were available.
- *Chapman's Fruit Shop* where jellies, ices, marmalades, cakes, liqueurs and other delicious things were sold in the highest state of perfection. (Rylance, 2012)

United States

Establishments selling ice cream were not confined to Europe. Enterprising confectioners made their way to New York City to open ice cream parlors in the United States.

Sources disagree on whom to credit with establishing the first ice cream parlor in the U.S. Some cite Giovanni Bosio, an Italian ice cream maker, with opening the first New York City gelateria in 1770. Unfortunately little documentation exists for this claim.

A better documented claim is that of Philip Lenzi, a confectioner from London. His arrival from London was announced in the November 25, 1773 edition of *Rivington's New York Gazetteer.*

Just arrived from London, Monsieur Lenzi, Confectioner. Makes and sells all sorts of fine French, English, Italian and German biskets, preserved fruits; also in brandy, jams, pastes, and jellies, which will be warranted for two or three years, with good care; all sorts of sugar plumbs, dragees, barley sugar, white and brown sugar candy, ice cream and fruits, sugar ornaments which will soon be ready for sale, or to lend out, with many other articles in all the greatest perfection, which he will sell and the most reasonable rates, he being content with a moderate profit, and spares no cost or pains to have every thing of the very best quality. He will undertake to furnish any public entertainment, as he has had the management of several given at Balls, Masquerades, &c. in most of the principal cities of Europe. He hopes for the countenance and encouragement of the public, which he will ever gratefully acknowledge. His arriving here so late in the season has prevented him from laying in to a great stock of fruits, &c. as he would otherwise have done. He will reside at the house of Mr. Richard Waldron, near the Exchange, till he can get a house more suitable for his business

.

---advertisement, *Rivington's New York Gazetteer*, November 25, 1773 (p. 4) (in Olver, 22004)

Four years later, this advertisment for Lenzi's shop appears in the *New-York Gazette, and Weekly Mercury*, May 12, 1777.

Philip Lenzi, Confectioner from London, Having removed from Dock-street to Hanover-Square, No. 517. Takes this method to return his sincere thanks to all his friends and customers for their past favours, and hopes for a continuance, and will have in this present season, a very great variety of the best sweetmeats; preserves marmelades, jellies, &c. in brandy, and very reasonable rate as the times will permit, for ready money only; and every thing of the said branch will be executed to all perfection as in the first shops in London. Said Lenzi

will, in the ensuing season, give a very good price for the very best sort of fruit, such as strawberries, gooseberries, cherries, raspberries, peaches, pine apples, green gages, apricots, &c. & c. May be had almost every day, ice cream; likewise ice for refreshing wine, &c. N.B. Wanted to said business, and apprentice---Premium is expected.
---advertisement, *New-York Gazette, and Weekly Mercury,* May 12, 1777 (p. 3)(in Olver, 22004)

By the 1780's, it appears that ice cream had gained a foothold in New York as ads began to appear for Lenzi's competitors. Not that that surprises anyone. Because, well ... ice cream!

As the ice trade expanded in the early eighteen hundreds, ice cream became cheaper to make. Ice cream street vendors proliferated during the Victorian era, making ice cream accessible to nearly all classes.

U is for Unmolding the ices for all to behold

U is for Unmolding the ices for all to behold.
Look at such beauty—it never gets old

Once ice cream had been made, there were two ways to present it to the dining table: rough and molded. Rough simply meant that it was soft frozen and put in a special serving vessel, the ice cream pail or *seau à glace*, designed to keep it cold, and taken to the dining table in that form to be scooped out and served. This "rough" presentation would have been the mostly like kind seen at pastry-shops and tea houses that some of Austen's character's visited.

Molds allowed for all manner of artistic creations and incredible presentations fit for fancy tables and special meals. They became so wildly popular that by 1830, ice cream pails were no longer being manufactured. (Day, 2004)

Ice Cream Molds

Ice cream molds were usually made of lead or pewter. Their forms ranged from a simple brick shape used for Neapolitan ice creams to elaborate towers, animals, even shapes that mimicked cuts of meat. (I read of a pig's head mold, filled with blood red ice cream to mimic meat. (Duggins, 2018) Sounds like a winner for my next dinner party for sure!) Fruits and vegetable were common themes. Flowers, biscuit, cigar and cheese-shaped molds were also very popular. Emy (1768) emphasized the use of these particular mold shapes, even calling some of his recipes *fromage* to imply the cheese shape of the mold rather than the flavor of the ice cream. (That is not to say the he didn't also have recipes for cheese ice cream, which he did.)

These molded ice creams were often colored with edible pigments, derived from cochineal, spinach, saffron and the like, before freezing. Powder colors were often painted onto the inside of the molds before the ice cream mixture was spooned in. Once the ice was unmolded, it might be painted with "edible" lead oxide or sulfur to further decorate it. Apparently those were considered edible in the day. (Dugggins, 2015) Leaves, stalks, even glass eyes for animal forms, might also be added to make the molds look realistic. It was all about the presentation.

The popularity of these shaped ices continued well into the twentieth century, until concern with a possible threat to health from the lead in the molds (and in the paints—yikes!) resulted in a sharp decline in their popularity. (*Feast for the Eyes,* Day, 2004)

No. 30.—CUCUMBER.

12⅜ inches long, 13s. 6d. each.

No. 31.—ASPARAGUS.

8¼ inches long, 3s. each.

No. 32.—GARNISHING OR DESSERT ICE MOULDS.
Grapes, Lemon, Artichoke, Gherkin, Strawberry, Peach, Plum, Pear,
Currant, Corn, Orange, Apricot, Fish, Oyster, Duck, Apple,
and many others.

1s. 9d. each.

Molding Ice Cream

After the ice cream had been initially soft frozen (congealed) in the sabotiere, it might be placed in a lead or pewter mold. The molds were often two pieced hinged affairs, held together by long metal pins. The seams of the mold had to be sealed with lard, butter or even wax in hopes of keeping out the salt water. (Illustration from Marshalls, 1888) Afterwards, the filled molds would be wrapped in brown paper to prevent ice from freezing to them. Then they would be submerged in a mixture of ice and salt for several hours until frozen hard. (Day, 2013)

Once frozen, the mold would be dipped ever so briefly in cold water to release the contents. At this point they would either be decorated and served, or stored until serving time. Borella (1777) details the process for us.

THE WAY TO MOULD ICES; IN ALL SORTS OF FRUITS.

When your composition is perfectly congealed (*your ice cream is soft frozen to the consistency of butter*) , take a spoon and the moulds you want to make use of; fill these well with your ices as quickly and dexterously as you can: you must have besides just ready by you a bucket with pounded natural ice, and a great deal of salt; there you put your moulds in proportion as you fill them, and cover them directly with pounded ice and salt, continuing so doing to every mould you fill up till you have filled them all. When that is done you cover them quite and set them a full hour in that ice.

When you want to take off what is in your moulds, you take a pan of water, and first wash well those moulds one after the other to rub off all the salt which sticks round them, then you open your moulds put their contents in a china dish and send them up.

You may give to every one of your ices the very colour of the fruit they represent; but then you must have your colour ready by you, and with a very fine pencil point them quickly, in which case they must likewise be served directly, or at least you must put them in the cave; then your cave must have been set in a bucket and prepared half an hour before you-take your fruits from their moulds: in that cave you are then to set them after they are coloured, till the moment comes of serving them; your fruit is certainly finer and takes the downy look of the natural one, (Borella, 1777)

Ice Caves

The cave Borella refers to is a pewter box which held the molded ice creams which was sealed and plunged into bucket of salt and ice.

The Victorian era saw an improvement on the traditional cave, with a device marketed as an ice cave. And ice cave was a double-walled metal box. Ice, salt and water would be placed between the walls to cool the interior to subfreezing temperatures. Essentially an early refrigerator, it could be used to freeze the molds (or to chill other foods), avoiding the problem of water seepage into the molds. Definitely an improvement to the earlier method, if you ask me. (Illustration from Marshall, 1888)

Somehow it's not surprising that A.B. Marshall held the patent for an ice cave (in addition to her nifty hand-crank ice cream freezer). She offered these directions for use:

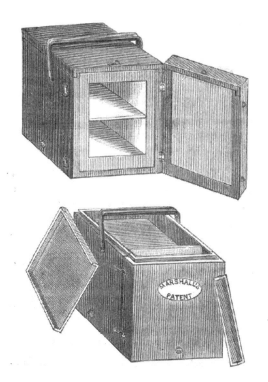

MOULDING AND KEEPING ICES.

Take a patent cave and remove the lids as shown in the annexed engraving, and fill in between the metals with a mixture of 2 parts broken ice and 1part salt; shake it well down so that the mixture goes underneath the cupboard of the cave, and fill well up so that the lid will just slide over the ice and salt. Replace the lids.

Now fill your mould with the frozen cream from the freezer, and see that it is well pressed or shaken into the mould. Place the mould for 1½ to 2 hours in the cave; examine from time to time if you wish.

When you desire to turn the ice out of the mould, dip the mould for an instant in cold water and turn it out as you would a jelly. If you put the ice, when turned out, back into the cave and shut the door, it will keep its shape for many hours, so that ices can be prepared long before actually required; they have thus been kept from one day to another. When anything is freezing in the cave, do not open the door more often than necessary.

When the cave is done with, remove the brine and wash out with boiling water, and see that it is put away dry. (Marshall, 1888)

.

V is for Vanilla

V is for Vanilla, a rare orchid fruit.
So popular now, there's no substitute.

With more than 200 flavor compounds, vanilla is one of the most complex flavors (so much for vanilla being a "plain" flavor). Moreover, it is unique in that it does not cause palate fatigue, ensuring the first vanilla bite tastes as good as the last. Today it is one of the most popular flavors, so popular it has lost much of its mystique, becoming "plain old vanilla." But that hasn't always been the case.

The Vanilla Orchid

Vanilla beans come from the only orchid variety (out of 25,000) that creates edible fruit. (Sonde, 2016) The vanilla orchid flowers open only for a few hours one day a year. If pollinated, they produce long green pods, or beans, containing tiny seeds which must remain on the vine from six to

Epidendrum Vanilla.
Vanillie.

nine months to ripen. Afterwards, they are harvested by hand.

Fresh vanilla beans are essentially without taste or aroma. The vanillin within is only released after an extensive process which involves alternately drying and sweating the beans, then conditioning them for about three months. This processing (and the need for hand pollination) makes vanilla the second-most expensive spice in the world. (Saffron is the first.)

The Spread of Vanilla

Vanilla (and chocolate) was first discovered, cultivated and prepared by the ancient peoples of Mexico. The Spanish, who conquered those lands in the sixteenth century, were the first Europeans to appreciate vanilla. For many decades thereafter, the Spanish controlled vanilla production and trade. (Kane, July 9, 2018)

Cortés brought vanilla back to Europe as a flavoring for Mexican hot drinking chocolate at Queen Elizabeth I's court. In 1602, her apothecary Hugh Morgan introduced sweets flavored primarily with vanilla on its own. The Queen's fondness for them ensured the spread of vanilla into a wide range of products including perfumes, tobacco and alcohol.

Vanilla was known in Regency England, but it was rare, expensive and seldom-used. It would remain so until after an 1841 advance in manual pollination that made it more readily available. By the middle of the nineteenth century, vanilla recipes were common. During the Regency, rose water was a far more common flavor for desserts and other sweets, while vanilla was more widely considered a flavoring for drinking chocolate. (Kane, July 9, 2018) So, Jane Austen probably never experienced the joys of vanilla ice cream.

Vanilla came late to English recipe books. Borella's, Clermont's and Nutt's cookbooks from the late 1770's and early 1800's contain no mention of vanilla ices or ice creams. Emy's 1768 cookbook featured several recipes for vanilla-flavored iced treats, but food historian Waverley Root suggests the first known recipe published in English featuring vanilla appears in the 1805 edition of Hannah Glasse's *The Art of Cookery*, which suggested adding "vanelas" to cacao beans prepared for drinking chocolate. (Rupp, 2014).

Thomas Jefferson

The lack of published English-language recipes for vanilla treats did not stop Thomas Jefferson from bringing back a recipe for vanilla ice cream acquired on his trip to Paris as Ambassador to France in 1784-1789. Thus, it appears he introduced the United States to vanilla.

JEFFERSON'S VANILLA ICE CREAM RECIPE

Take 2 of bottles cream, 6 egg yolks, ½ lb. sugar and a stick of vanilla cook over a fire, strain, pour into a sabotiere and set in a bucket of ice and salt. After 7 minutes, turn the sabotiere for 10 minutes, open and use a spatula used to loosen ice from the sides. Repeat several times until the ice cream [is] formed, then place in molds and pound down solid. (Reber, 2014)

Compare this to Emy's recipe from the same period:

VANILLA ICE CREAM

Finely grind a stick of vanilla with sugar until it will pass through a silk cloth. Four egg whites, beaten stiffly, can optionally be added. Add to a pint of double cream and add powdered sugar. (Translation by David Young.)

Somehow, passing it all through a silk cloth makes it all seem far more refined and better suited to a flavor of vanilla's distinction.

Food historian Karen Hess suggests Mary Randolph's *The Virginia Housewife* (1824) offers the first American recipe for vanilla ice cream (Rupp, 2014).

VANILLA CREAM.

Boil a vanilla bean in a quart of rich milk until it has imparted the flavour sufficiently; then take it out, and mix with the milk, eight eggs, yelks and whites, beaten well; let it boil a little longer--make it very sweet, for much of the sugar is lost in the operation of freezing.

And so vanilla quietly started its journey from exotic spice to just "plain old vanilla.".

W is for Wafers

W is for Wafers, crispy cookies to hold.
To put ice cream within them was really
quite bold.

I don't know about you, but it is hard to separate ice cream from ice cream cones. The two just go together so firmly in my mind that I almost never eat one without the other when I have the choice. But alas the ubiquitous pairing has been long in the making.

Did Jane Austen Eat Ice Cream Cones?

Culinary mythology suggests that though Jane Austen was likely to have enjoyed ice cream at some point in her life, she would never have even conceived of an ice cream cone.

It is suggested that ice cream cones were an invention of an ice cream vendor at a fair (possibly the 1904 World's Fair in St. Louis) in need of a way of serving their frozen treats. Who that ice cream vendor actually was and at what fair were they selling ice cream is a matter of some debate.

It doesn't take very long to fell that myth though. We know Italo Marchiony was granted a patent for a multiple cone mold on in December 15, 1903 so ice cream cones were clearly around before the 1904 fair.

But just how far back do ice cream cones go? That's where it all becomes rather interesting.

Wafers

Wafers, the stuff of which ice cream cones are made, date to the medieval era where they were an important part of a meal's end. Over the next few hundred years, they came to be regarded as "stomach settlers," served at the end to the meal to calm digestion. Eventually—because creative cooks just can't leave well enough alone don't you know—wafers transformed into luxurious treats, making up an important element of the dessert course. Rolled into three-dimensional shapes called funnels, cornucopias, horns or cornets they could be filled with all sort of fruit pastes, creams, and iced puddings—and chocolate, we must not forget the possibility of chocolate!

The first printed recipe for wafer cones is found Cleremont's *The Professed Cook* from 1769.

OF WAFERS AND OTHER PASTES.

The most fashionable are those made with

cream. Mix as much powder-sugar as good flour, with a little orangeflower water-; put this into a proper vessel, and pour some good cream to it by little and little, stirring it very well with a spoon to hinder it from forming into lumps, and add as much cream as will make the paste or batter pour out pretty thick from the spoon. This is also made with Spanish, or sweet wine: mix an equal weight of sugar-powder and flour as before, and work it with one or two new-laid eggs, and sweet wine sufficient to make the batter of the same consistence as the first. They are also done with butter: use the flour and sugar as usual, add a little rasped lemon-peel, and a few drops of orange-flower water; mix as before by degrees, with very good butter melted in a little milk until it comes to the same consistence as others: the paste being prepared after this manner, of either kind, warm the wafer iron on both sides, and rub it over with some butter tied in a linen bag, or a bit of virgin-wax; pour a spoonful of the batter, and bake over a smart fire, turning the iron once or twice until the wafer is done on both sides of a fine brown colour; if you would have them twisted, put them upon a mould ready at hand for that purpose; put it up directly as you take it out, and press it to the shape of whatever form you please, and so continue; always keep them in a warm place.

GAUFRES AU CAFFI. WAFERS, WITH COFFEE.

To a common table-spoonful of ground coffee, put a quarter of a pound of sugar-powder, and a quarter of a pound of fine flour; mix them well-with good thick cream as the preceding: yon may also put a little salt to either. (Cleremont, 1769)

From Wafers to Ice Cream Cones

One might note that Clermont does not actually talk about what to do with those cones once they are made. That was left entirely to the cook's imagination. It was not until Francatelli's *The Modern Cook* (1846) more than seventy five years later, that we see a specific recommendation that these wafer shapes be used to hold ice cream. He recommended filling the wafer cornets with ice cream and using them to garnish ice cream puddings, including the rather spectacular creation Iced Pudding à la Chesterfield.

ICED PUDDING, À LA CHESTERFIELD.

Grate one pound of pine-apple into a basin, add this to eight yolks of eggs, one pint and a half of boiled cream, one pound of sugar, and a very little salt; stir the whole together in a stewpan over a stove-fire until the custard begins to thicken; then pass it through a tammy, by rubbing with two wooden spoons, in the same manner as for a purée, in order to force the pine-apple through the tammy. This custard must now be iced in the usual manner, and put into a mould of the shape represented in the annexed wood cut; and in the centre of the iced cream, some macédoine ice of red fruits, consisting of cherries, currants, strawberries and raspberries in a cherry-water ice, must be introduced; cover the whole in with the lid, then immerse the pudding in rough ice in

the usual way, and keep it in a cool place until wanted. When about to send the pudding to table, turn it out of the mould on to its dish, ornament the top with a kind of drooping feather, formed with green angelica cut in strips, and arranged as represented in the wood-cut; *garnish the base with small gauffres, filled with some of the iced cream reserved for the purpose,* place a strawberry on the top of each, and serve. (Emphasis added)

Were there Ice Cream Cones in the Regency?

But I'm pretty sure that someone must have made the leap to use wafer cornets for ice cream in that seventy-five year gap between Cleremont's book and Francatelli's. In fact, near the end of the Regency era, in *The Italian Confectioner* (1820), G. A. Jarrin "wrote, that his almond wafers should be rolled 'on pieces of wood like hollow pillars, or give them any other form you may prefer. These wafers may be made of pistachios, covered with currants and powdered with coarse sifted sugar; they are used to garnish creams; when in season, a strawberry may be put into each end, but it must be a fine' . . . He suggested turning another of his wafers into 'little horns; they are excellent to ornament a cream." (Quinzio, 2000) Sounds like an ice cream filled cone to me!

Of course, that is only supposition, not concrete evidence. But fear not, we do have some tangible indication that ice cream cones might have been publicly consumed as early as 1807.

A colored engraving, titled *Frascati*, by Parisian Louis-Philibert Debucourt (1755-1832) published in 1807, depicted a Parisian café where at "small table in the right hand corner of the engraving with two ladies and a gentleman. On the table is a carafe and a glass, and the buxom lady facing us appears to be eating out of a cone which she is holding in her right hand. The gesture is modern and familiar to all of us ice cream cone consumers in the 21st century: cone slightly tipped, mouth open for a lick. Anyone would recognize this as an ice cream cone." (Weir, 2004)

So, did Jane Austen eat ice cream cones? We'll probably never know for sure, and all in all, it is unlikely, but it is just possible that she might have..

X is for Cautions, the infirm beware

X is for Cautions, the infirm beware:
Partake in that ice cream if only you dare.

With the popularity of ice cream, you know someone would have to come up with some kind of health warning, right? You know the more things change, the more they stay the same and all that. Well right from the beginning, someone did. In the sixteenth century, a significant percentage of physicians and other wise folk, who believed that adding snow or ice to drinks was a decadent practice which could lead to convulsions, colic, paralysis, blindness, madness and even sudden death. (Kane, Aug 9, 2013) While not everyone agreed with such a dire pronouncement, the notion did proliferate into the modern age.

This from Mrs. Beeton's (Victorian) book of *Household Management*:

The aged, the delicate and children should abstain

from ices or iced beverages; even the strong and healthy should partake of them in moderation. They should be taken immediately after the repast, or some hours after, because the taking these substances during the process of digestion is apt to provoke indisposition. It is necessary to abstain from them when persons are very warm or immediately after taking violent exercise as in some cases they have produced illnesses which have ended fatally. (Beeton, 1861)

No doubt Mr. Woodhouse (*Emma*) would not approve of ice cream at all. Better stick with a safe gruel instead.

Y is for yolk of so many eggs

Y is for yolks of so many eggs.
After eating all these, you best stick to veg.

Who doesn't love a rich ice cream? Is it possible to make an ice cream too rich? Take a look and decide for yourself. These are some of the richest recipes of the era, laden with many egg yolks and plenty of cream.

Topping the list with a dozen egg yolks to a pint of cream, the winners are:

CHEESE AS ICED BUTTER. FRONTAGE DE BEURRE GLACE.

Boil a pint of good cream a few minutes, with rasped lemon-peel, and a good spoonful of orange-flower water; when taken off the fire, add one dozen of yolks of eggs well beat up, and mix together without boiling; sift through a sieve, and put into an icing pot to freeze, working it like ices; ice it in such a manner that you may take it with a spoon to serve like pats of butter stamped, and bits of clean ice between to appear as crystals. (Clermont, 1776)

ROYAL ICE CREAM.

Take the yolks of ten eggs and two whole eggs, beat them up well with your spoon ; then take the rind of one lemon, two gills of syrup, one pint of cream, a little spice, and a little orange flower water ; mix them well and put them over the fire, stirring them all the time with your spoon ; when you find it grows thick take it off, and pass it through a sieve; put it into a freezingpot, freeze it, and take a little citron, and lemon and orange peel with a few pistachio nuts blanched; cut them all and mix them with your ice before you put them, in your moulds. (Nutt, 1807)

First runners up with ten egg yolks to a pint and a half of cream. (Yes, they are Victorian, but you'll humor me, right?):

ITALIAN CREAM ICE

Scald 1½ pints of cream or milk, with a little lemon peel and cinnamon, and mix it on to 10 raw yolks of eggs ; sweeten with 6 ounces of castor sugar (*superfine, but not powdered sugar*); thicken over the fire, tammy (*sieve*), and flavour, when cool, with a large wine-glassful of pale brandy, half a glass of noyeau, (*a liquor made from the intense bitter almond-flavored kernel found inside the pits of apricots and other stone fruits, also used to flavor the brandy based amaretto*) and the juice of 1 lemon. Freeze, and serve as in previous recipes. (Marshall,1888)

LEMON CREAM ICE (CRIME DE CITRON).

Peel 6 lemons very thinly, and put this peel to boil, with 1½ pints of cream or milk and 5 ounces of sugar, for 10 minutes ; then mix on to 10 raw yolks of eggs, and thicken over the fire and pass through the tammy (*sieve*). When cool add the juice from the lemons, which must be strained, and freeze. (Marshall,1888)

And the second runner up, named thusly since it only recommends a pint and a half of milk, not cream, to ten egg yolks:

RATAFIA CREAM ICE (CREME AU RATA-FIA).

Bruise 1 pound of ratafia biscuits (an almond-flavored cookie like a small macaroon) in the mortar. Make a custard of 1½ pints of milk, 10 raw yolks, and 6 ounces of sugar; and when it thickens, pour it over the bruised biscuits, and pass altogether through the tammy or hair sieve. Add half a wine-glass of noyeau syrup, and freeze. (Marshall,1888)

Finally honorable mention has to go to what amounts to hard-boiled egg ice cream by Emy

(1768, translation by David Young).

EGG ICE CREAM

When the cream base is half thickened, crumble in cooked egg yolks, eight per pint of cream. Continue (as with other ice creams).

(In all fairness, though, I should note, an egg is not an egg is not an egg. Historically eggs were much smaller until the 1930 when changes in feeding and breeding amped up the size. The general suggestion is that one modern egg equal two old fashioned eggs. So perhaps these recipes were not *quite* as rich as they looked at first glance. But still, hard-boiled egg ice cream?).

Z is for zenith

Z is for zenith, where angels abound,
to bring you ice cream high above the ground.

There is little doubt of what Emy (1768) thought about ice cream. The front piece of his book features angels (putti) making ice cream. Going clockwise from the middle right, a wheelbarrow loaded with ice is wheeled from an ice house. Slightly below and to the right, a putto crushes the ice in a large bucket. Another putto spins the inner vessels of the sabotiere containing ice cream mixtures that sit in buckets filled with crushed ice and salt. To the left, putti scoop the frozen ice cream from the sabotiere into ice cream glasses. At the top center, a tray of ice cream glasses is on its way to be served. I leave you with this image of ice cream as a heavenly experience.

L'Art de bien faire les Glaces

Recipe Index

References

"No One Does Feasting Like the Tudors." Hampton Court Palace. Accessed July 3001, 2018. https://www.hrp.org.uk/hampton-court-palace/no-one-does-feasting-like-the-tudors/#gs.KjaLHPM

Andrews, T. *Nectar and Ambrosia: An Encyclopedia of Food in World Mythology*. Oxford: ABC Clio, 2001.

Ashmole, Elias. *The Institution, Laws & Ceremonies of the Most* Noble *Order of the Garter.* London: Printed by J. Macock, for Nathanael Brooke ..., 1672.

Austen, Jane, and Laura Engel. *Sense and Sensibility*. New York: Barnes & Noble Classics, 2003.

Austen, Jane. *Pride and Prejudice*. New York: Tor, 1988.

Austen, Jane, and Margaret Drabble. *Emma*. New York, NY: Signet Classic, 1996.

Austen, Jane, Terry Castle, and John Davie. *Northanger Abbey ; Lady Susan ; The Watsons ; Sanditon*. Oxford: Oxford University Press, 1990.

Austen, Jane, Marilyn Butler, and James Kinsley. *Mansfield Park*. Oxford: Oxford University Press, 1990.

Austen, Jane, Claude Julien. Rawson, and John Davie. *Persuasion*. Oxford: Oxford University Press, 1990.

Ayto, John. *An A-Z of Food and Drink*. Oxford: Oxford University Press, 2002.

Bourne, Joanna. "What a pity it isn't illegal . . . Regency Ice Cream." Word Wenches. October, 2010 Accessed June 15, 2018. http://wordwenches.typepad.com/word_wenches/2010/10/regency-ice-cream.html

Capatti, Alberto & Massimo Montanari. *Italian Cuisine: A Cultural History*. Columbia University Press: New York, 1999.

Capatti, Alberto, and Massimo Montanari. *Italian Cuisine: A Cultural History*. Columbia University Press: New York, 1999.

Cole, Caroline. "'Twas Brilig! The Jabberwocky Ice Pail." MFAH. November 17, 2011. Accessed June 10, 2018. https://www.mfah.org/blogs/behind-scenes-rienzi/twas-brilig-case-study-jabberwocky-ice-pail

David, Elizabeth. *Harvest of the Cold Months: The Social History of Ice and Ices*. Viking: New York, 1994.

Davidson, Alan. *The Oxford Companion to Food*. Oxford: Oxford University Press, 1999.

Day, Ivan. "A Feast for the Eyes." Historic Food. 2004. Accessed June 20, 2018. http://www.historicfood.com/afeast_for_the_eyes.htm .

Day, Ivan. "Asparagus Ices." Historic Food. 2004. Accessed July 8, 2018. http://www.historicfood.com/Ice_Cream_Recipes.htm .

Day, Ivan. "Georgian Ices." Historic Food. 2004. Accessed June 18, 2018. http://www.historicfood.com/Georgian Ices.htm .

Day, Ivan. "Wafer Making." Historic Food. 2004. Accessed June 21, 2018. http://www.historicfood.com/Wafer.htm .

Day, Ivan. "Lady Ann Fanshawe's Icy Cream." Food History Jottings. April 5, 2012. Accessed June 1, 2018. http://foodhistorjottings.blogspot.com/2012/04/lady-anne-fanshawes-icy-cream.html .

Day, Ivan. "Mr. Agnes Marshall's Cucumber Ice creams." Food History Jottings. December 11, 2013. Accessed June 1, 2018 http://foodhistorjottings.blogspot.com/2013/12/mrs-agnes-marshalls-cucumber-ice-creams.html.

Dickson, Paul. *The Great American Ice Cream Book*. Atheneum:New York,1972

Drawing, A Covered Dish for Ice Cream of Porcelain, 1775–1800. 1775–1800. Drawings, Prints, and Graphic Design, Cooper Hewitt, Smithsonian Design Museum. In *Wikimedia*. December 3, 2017. Accessed June 3, 2018. https://commons.wikimedia.org/wiki/File:Drawing,_A_covered_dish_for_ice_cream_of_porcelain,_1775–1800_(CH_18117443).jpg.

Duggins, Alexi. "Would you eat ice cream from 300 years ago?" The Telegraph. August 20, 2015. accessed July 10, 2018. https://www.telegraph.co.uk/foodanddrink/fo

odanddrinknews/11811900/Would-you-eat-ice-cream-from-300-years-ago.html

Hess, Karen. (transcriber) *Martha Washington's Booke of Cookery*. Columbia University Press: New York, 1981.

Inglis-Arkell, Esther. "How Did They Make Ice Cream in the 17th Century?" Gizmodo. December 29, 2015. Accessed July 5, 2018. https://gizmodo.com/how-did-they-make-ice-cream-in-the-17th-century-1749823474 .

Kane, Kathryn. "Before Vanilla: Rose Water in the Regency." The Regency Redingote. May, 4, 2018. Accessed July 9, 2018. https://regencyredingote.wordpress.com/2018/05/04/before-vanilla-rose-water-in-the-regency/

Kane, Kathryn. "Frigorific Solutions of the Regency " Regency Redingote. 16 August 2013. Accessed July 10, 2018. https://regencyredingote.wordpress.com/2013/08/16/frigorific-solutions-of-the-regency/

Kane, Kathryn. "Regency Chocolate—Pale, Thick and Frothy." Regency Redingote. May, 13, 2018. Accessed July 8, 2018. http://regencyredingote.wordpress.com/2011/05/13/regency-chocolate-mdash-pale-thick-and-frothy/

Kane, Kathryn. "Saltpetre: Regency Refrigeration" Regency Redingote. 9 August 2013. Accessed July 10, 2018. https://regencyredingote.wordpress.com/2013/08/09/saltpetre-regency-refrigeration/

Kraft, Amy. "Here's How Ice Cream Was Made in the 1800s." Modern Notion. August 21, 2014. Accessed June 12, 2018. http://modernnotion.com/heres-ice-cream-made-1800s/ .

Lee, Vivien. "The Epic, Sensational, Anything-But-Plain Story of Vanilla." Super Call. September, 18, 2017. Accessed July 9, 2018. https://www.supercall.com/culture/history-of-vanilla-the-secretly-insane-origin-of-vanilla

Leslie, Ellen. "The ice house uncovered" Country Life. October 4, 2010 . Accessed, March 20, 2014. http://www.countrylife.co.uk/comment-opinion/the-ice-house-uncovered-20789#Fbm1KZheZ6tZ1KhX.99

Mariani, John. *The Dictionary of Italian Food and Drink*. Broadway Books: New York, 1998.

Olver, Lynne. "Food Timeline FAQs: Ice Cream & Ice." Food Timeline. 2004. Accessed June 8, 2018. http://www.foodtimeline.org/foodicecream.html.

Quinzio, Jeri. "Asparagus Ice Cream, Anyone?" Gastronomica. May 05, 2002. Accessed June 12, 2018. https://gastronomica.org/2002/05/05/asparagus-ice-cream-anyone.

Quinzio, Jeri. *Of Sugar and Snow: A History of Ice Cream Making*. University of California Press: Berkeley 2009.

Quinzio, Jeri. "Ice Cream Cone Conundrum," Radcliffe Culinary Times, Vol. X, No. 1, Spring 2000, Radcliffe Culinary Friends of the

Schesinger Library, the *Radcliffe* Institute for Advanced Study, Harvard University.

Randolph, Mary and Karen Hess. *The Virginia Housewife*. Facsimile 1824 edition with historical notes and commentaries by Karen Hess. University of South Carolina Press: Columbia SC, 1984.

Reber, Patricia Bixler. "Mary Randolph's Peach Ice Cream." Researching Food History. August 21, 2017. Accessed June 8, 2018. http://researchingfoodhistory.blogspot.com/2017/08/mary-randolphs-peach-ice-cream.html

Reber, Patricia Bixler. "Thomas Jefferson and Ice Cream." Researching Food History. July 28, 2014. Accessed June 8, 2018. http://researchingfoodhistory.blogspot.com/2014/07/thomas-jefferson-and-ice-cream.html

Rossen, Jake. "A Cool History of Ice Cream." Mental Floss. June 28, 2017. Accessed June 20, 2018. http://mentalfloss.com/article/502325/cool-history-ice-cream.

Rupp, Rebecca. "The History of Vanilla." National Geographic. October 23, 2014. Accessed July 9, 2018. https://www.nationalgeographic.com/people-and-culture/food/the-plate/2014/10/23/plain-vanilla/The History of Vanilla

Rylance, Ralph. Janet Ing Freeman, ed. *The Epicure's Almanac: Eating and Drinking in Regency London*. The British Library: London. 2012.

Sanborn, Vic. "The Pot and Pineapple and Gunter's: Domenico Negri, Robert Gunter, and the Confectioner's Art in Georgian London." Jane Austen's World. July 10, 2013. Accessed June 8, 2018.

https://janeaustensworld.wordpress.com/2013/07/09/the-pot-and-pineapple-and-gunters-domenico-negri-robert-gunter-and-the-confectioners-art-in-georgian-london/.

Sanborn, Vic. "Storing Ice and Making Ice Cream in Georgian England." Jane Austen's World. September, 29, 2008. Accessed June 5, 2018. https://janeaustensworld.wordpress.com/2008/09/29/storing-ice-and-making-ice-cream-in-georgian-england/ .

Simeti, Mary Taylor. *Pomp and Sustenance: Twenty-Five Centuries of Sicilian Food*. Ecco Press: Hopewell NJ, 1989.

Sonde, Kari. "A Brief History of Ice Cream Flavors." First We Feast. Jul 8, 2016. Accessed July 9, 2018. https://firstwefeast.com/eat/2016/07/ice-cream-flavor-history

Stradley, Linda. "History Of Ice Cream Cone." What's Cooking America. February 20, 2017. Accessed June 10, 2018. https://whatscookingamerica.net/History/IceCream/IceCreamCone.htm

Stradley, Linda. "Legends and Myths of Ices and Ice Cream History." What's Cooking America. January 05, 2017. Accessed June 12, 2018. https://whatscookingamerica.net/History/IceCream/IceCreamHistory.htm.

Thomson, J., and Adolphe Smith. *Street Life in London*. London: Sampson Low, Marston, Searle and Rivington, 1877.

Upton, Emly. "The History of Ice Cream." Today I Found Out. June 16, 2013. Accessed June 10, 2018. http://www.todayifoundout.com/index.php/2013/06/the-history-of-ice-cream/ .

Walton, Geri. "What are Cellars, Storage, and Out-buildings?" Geri Walton. July 6, 2015. Accessed July 7, 2015 https://www.geriwalton.com/what-are-cellars-storage-and/

Weir, Robert J. "An 1807 Ice Cream Cone: Discovery and Evidence." Historic Food. Accessed June 21, 2018. http://www.historicfood.com/Ice Cream Cone.htm .

A Lady. *Domestic Economy and Cookery for the rich and poor*. London: Longman, Rees, Orme, Brown and Green. 1827.

Beeton, Isabella. *Beeton's Book of Household Management*. London: S. O. Beeton Publishing, 1861.

Borella. *The Court and Country Confectioner: Or, the House-keepers Guide ; to a More Speedy, Plain, and Familiar Method of Understanding the Whole Art of Confectionary ... A New Edition. To Which Is Added, a Dissertation on the Different Species of Fruits, and the Art of Distilling ... By Mr. Borella ..*London: Printed for G. Riley, 1772.

Briggs, Richard. *The New Art of Cookery; According to the Present Practice: Being a Complete Guide to All Housekeepers, on a Plan Entirely New; Consisting of Thirty-eight Chapters. ... With Bills of Fare for Every Month in the Year, Neatly and Correctly Printed.*Philadelphia:: Printed for H. & P. Rice, and Sold by J. Rice and Baltimore., 1798.

Clermont, B., and Menon. *The Professed Cook ; Or, the Modern Art of Cookery, Pastry, and Confectionary, Made Plain and Easy ... including a Translation of Les Soupers De La Cour ... By B. Clermont ... The Third Edition, Revised and Much Enlarged*. London: W. Davis, Etc., 1776.

Cooke, John Conrade. *Cookery and confectionery.* London : W. Simpkin, and R. Marshall, 1824.

Eales, Mary. *Mrs. Mary Eales's Receipts: Confectioner to Her Late Majesty Queen Anne.* London: 1733 (first ed. 1718)

Emy, M. *L'Art de bien faire les glaces d'office; ou Les vrais principes pour congeler tous les rafraichissemens.* Paris, 1768.

Francatellli, Charles Elme'. *The Modern Cook: A Practical Guide to the Culinary Art in All Its Branches, Comprising, in Addition to English Cookery, the Most Approved and Recherche' Systems of French, Italian, and German Cookery ; Adapted as Well for the Largest Establishments as for the Use of Private Families..* London, New Burlington Street: Richard Bentley. 1846.

Gillier, Joseph. *Le Cannameliste Français* (1751). Reprint: *Nancy: Le veuve Leclerc, 1768.

Glasse, Hannah. *The Art of Cookery, Made Plain and Easy: Which Far Exceeds Any Thing of the Kind Ever Yet Published ...* London: Printed for the Author, and Sold at Mrs. Ashburn's, a China Shop, the Corner of Fleet-Ditch, 1784.

Goodfellow, Mrs. *Mrs. Goodfellow's Cookery As it Should Be: A New Manual of the Dining Room And Kitchen ...* Philadelphia: T. B. Peterson & brothers, 1865.

Marshall, A. B. Wheaton. *Mrs. A.B. Marshall's cookery book.* London : Simpkin, Marshall, Hamilton, Kent, & Co: Marshall's School of Cookery, 1890.

Marshall, A. B. Wheaton. *The Book of Ices*. London : Simpkin, Marshall, Hamilton, Kent, & Co: Marshall's School of Cookery, 1888.

Nutt, Frederick. *The Complete Confectioner; Or, the Whole Art of Confectionary: ... By a Person, Late an Apprentice to the Well-known Messrs. Negri and Witten.* London: Printed for the Author, 1807.

Putnam, Elizabeth H. *Mrs. Putnams Receipt Book: And Young Housekeeper's Assistant (classic Reprint).* Boston: Ticknor, Reeds and Fields. 1853

Raffald, Elizabeth. *The Experienced English Housekeeper*. London: R, Baldwin, 1769.

Rundell, Maria Eliza Ketelby. *A New System of Domestic Cookery: Formed upon Principles of Economy, and Adapted to the Use of Private Families*. A New ed. London: Printed for John Murray ..., 1814.

Acknowledgments

So many people have helped me along the journey taking this from an idea to a reality.

Julie, , Anji, and Debbie hank you so much for cold reading, proof reading and being honest! Thanks to David young for his assistance with translating Emy into modern English.

And my dear friend Cathy, my biggest cheerleader, you have kept me from chickening out more than once!

And my sweet sister Gerri who believed in even those first attempts that now live in the file drawer!

Thank you!

Other Books by Maria Grace

Remember the Past
The Darcy Brothers

A Jane Austen Regency Life Series:
A Jane Austen Christmas: Regency Christmas Traditions
Courtship and Marriage in Jane Austen's World
How Jane Austen Kept her Cook: An A to Z History of Georgian Ice Cream

Jane Austen's Dragons Series:
A Proper Introduction to Dragons
Pemberley: Mr. Darcy's Dragon
Longbourn: Dragon Entail
Netherfield:Rogue Dragon

The Queen of Rosings Park Series:
Mistaking Her Character
The Trouble to Check Her
A Less Agreeable Man

Sweet Tea Stories:
A Spot of Sweet Tea: Hopes and Beginnings (short story anthology)
A Spot of Sweet Tea: Christmastide Tales (Christmas novella anthology)

Snowbound at Hartfield
Darcy and Elizabeth: Christmas 1811
The Darcy's First Christmas
From Admiration to Love

On Line Exclusives at:

__www.http//RandomBitsofFascination.com__

Bonus and deleted scenes
Regency Life Series

__Free e-books__:
Bits of Bobbin Lace
The Scenes Jane Austen Never Wrote: First Anniversaries
Half Agony, Half Hope: New Reflections on Persuasion
Four Days in April
Jane Bennet in January
February Aniversaries

❦ About the Author

Though Maria Grace has been writing fiction since she was ten years old, those early efforts happily reside in a file drawer and are unlikely to see the light of day again. After penning five file-drawer novels in high school, she took a break from writing to pursue college and earn her doctorate in Educational Psychology. After 16 years of university teaching, she returned to her first love, fiction writing.

She has one husband and one grandson, two graduate degrees and two black belts, three sons, four undergraduate majors, five nieces, is has blogged six years on *Random Bits of Fascination*, has built seven websites, attended eight English country dance balls, sewn nine Regency era costumes, and shared her life with ten cats.

She can be contacted at:

author.MariaGrace@gmail.com

Facebook:
http://facebook.com/AuthorMariaGrace

On Amazon.com:
http://amazon.com/author/mariagrace

Random Bits of Fascination
(http://RandomBitsofFascination.com)

Austen Variations (http://AustenVariations.com)

English Historical Fiction Authors
(http://EnglshHistoryAuthors.blogspot.com)

White Soup Press (http://whitesouppress.com/)

On Twitter @WriteMariaGrace

On Pinterest:
http://pinterest.com/mariagrace423/

Printed in Great Britain
by Amazon